THAI COOKERY SECRETS

How to cook delicious curries and pad thai

THAI
COOKERY
SECRETS

HOW TO COOK DELICIOUS
CURRIES AND PAD THAI

Kris Dhillon

RIGHT WAY

Constable & Robinson Ltd
3 The Lanchesters
162 Fulham Palace Road
London W6 9ER
www.constablerobinson.com

Published by Right Way, an imprint of Constable & Robinson, 2010

A copy of the British Library Cataloguing in Publication Data
is available from the British Library

ISBN: 978-0-7160-2227-5

Printed and bound in the EU
3 5 7 9 10 8 6 4 2

CONTENTS

INTRODUCTION

Before the publication of *The Curry Secret* almost 20 years ago, the Indian restaurant curry was an enigma. An elusive and moreish flavour that almost everyone loved but few outside of the closed restaurant community knew how to produce. Indian restaurant cooking had become shrouded in mystique and secrecy and it was the exploration and de-mystification of those cooking processes that made *The Curry Secret* a bestseller.

It is not so with Thai 'restaurant cuisine' where the converse is true.

Thai restaurants in the western world barely capture the true essence of Thai food. The fresh, fragrant and intoxicating flavours of good Thai food are amazing taste sensations rarely replicated by the majority of Thai restaurants. Cooking fabulous Thai food need not be difficult, but it requires a commitment to really fresh, flavoursome ingredients, correctly combined and quickly cooked to retain all their wonderful colour, aroma and flavour. Too many Thai chefs in the west compromise with the quality and freshness of the ingredients or the way they are cooked so that much of those delicious, satisfying flavours typical of real Thai cuisine are lost.

To experience the best of Thai food, you have to cook it like they do in Thailand.

My interest in Thai food began almost a quarter of a century ago when I fell in love with the delicious, complex spicy flavours of Tom Yum Soup, skewered Sate Chicken and Thai Red Curry served in a well frequented Thai restaurant in Birmingham, England. Like most non-Thais, however, I found that many of the ingredients used to produce these flavours were a bit of a mystery and very difficult to source. Since then several trips to Bangkok's vibrant food scene have served to increase my understanding of and cement my relationship with Thai cuisine and, as Asian cuisines have become increasingly popular all over the world, many of the uniquely Thai ingredients are now much easier to find. Thai food still remains an enigma to many people though, and this book is written from the understanding of a 'non-Thai' for 'non-Thais' wishing to cook this wonderful food in their own kitchens.

It quickly becomes obvious to anyone visiting Thailand that food is central to the fabric of Thai society. For Thais, food is not just for eating. It is a reason for people to get together with friends, family and community in celebration and joy. In Thai culture, as in my own Indian culture, food is used for religious offerings and services, and leftovers are never wasted. To throw food away is, in Thailand, a sin punishable by 'the God of rice' with bad luck or famine.

Thai cuisine is colourful, fragrant, healthy and delicious and, to top it all, dishes are always beautifully presented. The concept of intricate and artistic presentation of food has been around for centuries in Thailand. It was first developed in the royal palaces where royal chefs had to make meals highly attractive as well as superbly delicious. Beautiful presentation has become an important aspect of Thai cuisine. Serving platters are often decorated with all manner of exquisitely carved fruits and vegetables, whilst palace-style stir-fries usually incorporate elegantly carved vegetables within the dish itself.

Traditional Thai cuisine consists of various types of meat and seafood combined with locally produced vegetables, herbs and spices always served with rice. Around the fourteenth century the Chinese introduced noodles and wok cooking to Thailand and, later, influences from neighbours such as Vietnam, Cambodia, Burma, Indonesia, Malaysia and others resulted in the modern-day complex flavours of Thai food.

India has also played a significant role in the evolution of Thai cuisine, but the majority of Thai curries remain quite different from Indian curries. Although some Indian spices are used in a minority of Thai dishes, Thai food has developed its unique flavour due to the use of local ingredients such as galangal (similar to ginger), lemongrass, kaffir lime and Thai holy basil.

Pad Thai, meaning 'Thai style frying', is a dish of stir-fried noodles with several other ingredients including egg, peanuts, shallots, bean sprouts, tofu and meat or seafood flavoured with lime or tamarind. Although the dish has been eaten in various forms throughout Thailand for centuries, Pad Thai as we know it today was purported to have been developed in Bangkok to serve busy office workers with a quick, nutritious and tasty meal during their lunch breaks. Whilst the best Pad Thai is still to be found at the food stalls of Bangkok's food markets, it is now one of the most popular Thai dishes in restaurants around the world, although this version tends to be oilier and heavier than the lighter Pad Thai found on the streets of Thailand.

Whilst the spectacularly fresh and complex flavours of Thai food cooked in Thailand may be near impossible to replicate perfectly elsewhere, there need not be any mystery about cooking delicious Thai food anywhere in the world. It is quite simple once you come to know the basic principles of Thai flavours and this book will show you how to get those wonderful flavours from locally produced and imported ingredients. It will also give you some nifty cooking techniques and lots of helpful tips to help make cooking great Thai food a breeze.

1

ABOUT THAI CURRIES

Curry in some form or another is popular throughout Asia and the Middle East. Thought to have its origins in India and Pakistan, curry was introduced to south-east Asia by Indian immigrants several centuries ago, where over time it underwent a period of evolution, changing and developing some unique characteristics with the inclusion of local ingredients and cooking styles.

Thai v Indian Curry

The typical Thai curry (*gaeng*) is quite different from Indian curry. The Thai curry is generally a speedily cooked more soup-like dish made with coconut milk or water with a complex and aromatic base of fresh curry paste, compared to its Indian counterpart which is often slow cooked with a thicker sauce made with a base of onion, ginger and dried spice blends. Also, Thai cooks use more fresh herbs (such as lemongrass, kaffir lime and basil) and rarely use the dried herbs and spices favoured by Indian cooks. On the whole there are very few Thai curries that resemble Indian curries. A couple of exceptions are the Massaman (Thai Muslim) and Panang curry – two Thai curries based predominantly on dried herbs and warm Indian style spices.

There are only four spices used regularly in Thai cooking. Dry roasted cumin and coriander seeds, turmeric and dried chilli are ground and combined in varying proportions with fresh herbs to make the pungent and beautifully aromatic curry pastes that are unique to Thai cooking. Indian cuisine, on the other hand, is characterized by the expert use of several spices and spice blends that include cardamom, fenugreek, mustard seed, cinnamon, nutmeg and many others.

Types of Thai Curry

In many Thai homes some type of spicy, aromatic curry is eaten with rice every day. Endless combinations of fresh and tasty ingredients go to make dozens of different types of delicious Thai curries, traditionally containing little meat. With local herbs and vegetables, some grown around the home, it is an economical, tasty and nutritious dish.

Thai curries can be broadly split into two categories – coconut based or water based – and further identified by the colour or type of curry paste used.

Coconut based Thai Curry

The richer coconut based Thai curries are the most popular in Thai restaurants throughout the west, with red (*gaeng phet*), green (*gaeng kiow whan*) and Massaman (*gaeng massaman*) being the most popular with western diners. Yellow Thai curry (*gaeng leuang*) and Panang (*gaeng phanaeng*) are also common. These curries, often made with generous amounts of coconut cream or milk, are deliciously creamy and generally less spicy, the coconut fat effectively toning down the heat of the chillies.

Water based Thai Curry

The spiciest Thai curries are generally water based. Water based sour curries (*gaeng sohm plah*), often prepared with fish and souring agents such as tamarind or lime, are typically eaten throughout Thailand. Jungle curry (*gaeng pah*), a delicious, spicy curry cooked with or without meat, is probably the best known water based curry in western restaurants. Water or stock based Thai soups are often eaten with rice or noodles in much the same way as curries.

Whether you choose to make your curries with water or coconut, how hot you choose to have them is purely a matter of personal taste and your own chilli tolerance. Varying the amount of chilli, using a milder variety of chilli, adding more coconut milk or cream, are all effective ways of moderating the heat of the Thai curry.

2

BASIC INGREDIENTS
FOR THAI FLAVOURS

The unique taste of Thai food comes with the harmonious melding of four main flavours – sweet, sour, salty and spicy-hot – underpinning the lively, fresh aromas and flavours produced by fresh herbs and vegetables. Good Thai cuisine is intensely flavoursome and incredibly delicious, so much so that eating a good Thai curry can lift your spirits and enhance your mood.

The best Thai cooking utilizes the freshest ingredients possible to produce wonderfully vibrant, fragrant and flavour packed dishes, but the secret of a really good Thai dish is in creating a balance between the four main flavours. Each flavour has to be intense enough to make a statement but not so strong that it overpowers the others. More about how to create this harmony of flavours is outlined further on in the book.

The basic ingredients used to produce the sweet, sour, salty and spicy flavours unique to Thai food are listed overleaf.

Although these ingredients are readily available in most places these days, you don't have to do without Thai food just because you can't find one or more of them where you live. The beauty of Thai cuisine is that it is quite adaptable and flexible so you can successfully substitute any of the ingredients listed here with other readily available items for similar results.

Fish sauce	*(nam pla)*	salty and pungent
Kaffir limes	*(ma gruud)*	sour and aromatic
Tamarind	*(ma kam piek)*	sour with a hint of sweetness
Lemongrass	*(ta krai)*	sour and aromatic
Palm sugar	*(nam taan peep)*	rich and sweet
Cumin	*(ye raa)*	spicy and aromatic
Ground pepper	*(prig thai bhon)*	spicy and hot
Ground chillies	*(prig kee nu bonn)*	very hot
Fresh Thai chillies	*(prik kee noo)*	hot (7/10) and aromatic

For instance, fish sauce can be substituted with light soy sauce or even salt. As fish sauce is quite pungent and not to everyone's taste some western cooks prefer to use soy sauce or salt instead anyway.

Kaffir limes, lemongrass and tamarind can be substituted with limes, lemons or even a little vinegar. I often use grated fresh lime zest and lime juice instead of kaffir lime, for impromptu and delicious Thai curries and soups.

Soft brown or white sugar can be used instead of palm sugar, and cumin may be substituted with coriander (seed) or left out altogether if neither was available. Even the chilli powder can be substituted with hot sauce if necessary.

Some ingredients like lemongrass and kaffir lime leaves may be available frozen so check the freezer section of your supermarket if you can't get them fresh. Whilst the frozen ingredients are quite good, in my experience the same ingredients in dried form are generally tasteless.

The key is to use fresh vegetables and herbs and authentic ingredients where you can, and substitute where you can't but also to cook Thai dishes according to your personal taste, tasting as you cook, and adding a little more of this or that until the balance of those four flavours feels just right to your tastebuds.

Other Important Ingredients for Thai cooking

There are many exotic, unusual and (in the west) unfamiliar ingredients used in traditional Thai cooking throughout Thailand. I have focused mainly on recipes that can be made with ingredients that are easily available just about everywhere, but I've also given some ideas on substituting in case you can't find something.

Fresh Ingredients

Coriander (Cilantro)	
Mint	
Galangal	use ginger instead
Thai chillies	use any chilli according to how hot you want it
Thai basil	use sweet basil instead
Thai holy basil	use sweet basil instead
Thai lemon basil	use lemon scented basil instead
Crispy fried garlic	omit or use crispy fried onion
Crispy fried onion	omit if not available
Bean sprouts	
Garlic	
Garlic shoots (flat garlic chives)	omit or grow your own
Shallots (French shallots)	cooking onion may be used instead
Spring onions (scallions)	
Thai eggplant	any aubergine (eggplant)

Dried Ingredients

Bay leaf
Cardamom
Cumin
Cloves
Coriander seeds
Turmeric
Paprika
Dried shrimps   omit if not available

Other Ingredients

Coconut milk   use canned in preference to powdered
Coconut cream   use canned in preference to powdered
Jasmine rice   any long-grain white rice
Rice noodles   fresh or dried
Shrimp paste
(Ka Pee or Belacan) omit if not available

3

HERBS IN THAI COOKING AND HOW TO GROW YOUR OWN

Fresh herbs are used liberally in Asian cooking, and Thai food is no exception to this. The colour, aroma and flavour that fresh herbs impart cannot be matched by anything else. Herbs like coriander, basil and mint are available everywhere nowadays which is just as well because no Thai dish would be complete without one or more of these lovely culinary wonders.

Most herbs are really easy to grow and can be grown in pots, hanging baskets, borders or beds. The sheer pleasure of picking your own, fresh, intoxicatingly aromatic herbs just when you need them is worth experiencing – and you can be sure that they are chemical-free and with no food miles.

To get the best possible flavour and aroma, always try to include as many as possible of the fresh herbs listed in a recipe for Thai food.

Coriander (Cilantro)
Coriander is an absolute must for Thai cooking, where not just the leaves but all parts of the plant are used in different preparations and stages of cooking. Coriander root is an essential ingredient for Thai curry pastes, the stems are added

to soups, curries and stir-fries and the leaves used for garnish and decoration.

Home-grown coriander, freshly picked, is the best for flavour and fragrance. It is easy to grow and can be grown year round in a warm climate and during the warmer months in cold climates. Soak a handful of coriander seeds (the same coriander seeds you use as a spice) in a little water overnight. The next day, spread the seeds onto well drained soil in a garden bed, or in a deep pot placed where it will get lots of sun. Cover with a light sprinkling of soil or compost and water in. Keep moist and the seeds will germinate in about 14 days. You can begin to harvest when the plants are as little as 10 cm (3 inches) high but they will grow to about double this height.

Coriander bolts and goes to seed quite quickly if it dries out or if the weather becomes hot. The green seeds are intensely aromatic and can be used for anything that you would use the fresh herb for.

Coriander is not a 'cut and come again' herb like mint or basil and will need to be sown every three to four weeks for a continuous supply.

Thai Basil, Thai Holy Basil and Thai Lemon Basil

These three varieties are quite different in appearance, aroma and flavour but all are interchangeable according to personal preference. Thai Basil has beautiful purple-green leaves and a mild aniseed flavour. Thai Holy Basil has large green leaves with purple stems and tastes more of cloves with a musky aroma that intensifies with cooking. Lemon Basil is a fast-growing plant with pale-green leaves and a fresh citrus aroma that is great with seafood dishes.

Basil is a popular herb in Thai cooking and there are several strains of oriental basils, all generally stronger in flavour than western varieties. These sensationally aromatic herbs make excellent pot plants that can be grown indoors (preferably with periods of sunshine in the open air) or outdoors during warm weather. Grow them as border plants or in pots and containers. They will do well in partial shade or full sun but they need a sheltered position and good drainage.

Sow seeds in late spring or early summer about 5mm (¼ inch) deep and about 30 cm (12 inches) apart where they are to grow, or buy seedlings or potted plants from your local nursery or garden centre. Pick the leaves as needed and remove flower heads to keep the plants growing vigorously.

Garlic Shoots (Flat Garlic Chives)

Garlic is used liberally in Thai cooking and, although the green shoots that appear when garlic cloves are planted are not absolutely essential, the best flavour, colour and aroma will be achieved if they are included in a recipe that calls for them. Many greengrocers and supermarkets sell them these days but why pay the extra when you can so easily grow your own and have the freshest garlic chives in your backyard just when you need them?

Garlic shoots are similar in appearance to the green shoots on spring onions only they are flat and not quite as dark green. They can be grown year round except in very cold climates when the ground is frozen. In cold climates, plant cloves from spring onwards for harvesting through summer and autumn, right through to about six weeks before the ground is expected to freeze for harvesting the following spring. To sow, simply insert unpeeled garlic cloves into free-draining soil, about 15 cm (6 inches) apart in pots or garden beds until just the very top is visible above the soil. Keep moist and harvest when the shoots are around 25 cm (10 inches) high. If you harvest by slicing off the green part about 2 cm (just under an inch) above the ground, it will sprout again at least two or three times before you have to start again.

Beware though. Much of the garlic available in the western world is imported and, as part of the regulatory process, it is irradiated and treated with chemicals and hormones. This treatment increases the shelf life of the garlic but also effectively kills it so it will not grow. My mother, who had been growing garlic all her life, spent several frustrated years trying to grow it in England only to find that she couldn't. The garlic either would not sprout shoots at all or, if it did, growth was stunted and useless. She had given up in despair until I realized what was going on and purchased some organically grown garlic bulbs which she hopefully, but sceptically, divided into cloves and planted in deep pots. Because the garlic was fresh and young, it took much longer to sprout than expected (during which time my mother totally gave up on the idea) but suddenly one day beautiful, healthy green shoots appeared all over the place. Needless to say, mum was ecstatic.

Planting it for garlic chives is a great way to use garlic cloves that are a bit old or starting to sprout, but, to be sure it will grow, you will need to buy organically or locally grown garlic that has not been destroyed with chemicals.

Spring Onions (Scallions) and Onion Shoots

These versatile little plants are used by cooks all over the world. Many western recipes call for the white part of the spring onion only but in Thai and other Asian cooking it is the green shoots that are most prized to add flavour, colour and aroma to a whole host of dishes. They are not an 'essential' but they do contribute that wow factor to many curries and soups.

Spring onions are readily available all year round, but home-grown produce is always fresher, costs next to nothing and is available just when you need it. Sow seeds thinly in rows in well-drained soil every three weeks or so from spring to autumn or buy onion sets for greater ease and speed to harvesting. Another way of obtaining fresh green onion shoots quickly and cheaply is to plant cooking onions that are beginning to sprout. Simply bury them in soil or compost, in pots or garden beds, leaving the shooting peak exposed above ground. Water occasionally and slice off shoots as you need them.

Mint (Spearmint)

One of the most wonderful of herbs, mint is popular all over the world. Nothing compares with its fresh, 'minty' flavour and aroma. It's fabulous in anything from sweets like chocolate to ice-cream and savoury concoctions like chutneys to sauces. It's also amazingly easy to grow; in fact, given half a chance, this hardy perennial will happily spread all over your garden.

Mint does not grow well from seed so either buy a plant from your local nursery or dig up a small piece of the plant – including some of the root – from a friend's or neighbour's crop. Choose a site in your garden where it can spread freely without interfering with other plants, or plant it in a good-sized pot. Another way to control mint's rampant habit is to plant it in a bottomless container sunk into the soil. I've grown mint this way for some years and it works really well.

Mint prefers partial shade and moist, reasonably rich soils, but it will grow in full sun or very little sun and in any kind of soil you have. Keep the soil moist until the plant is established and harvest often, whether you need it or not, to encourage vigorous growth. Prune back to just above ground level once the gardening season is over and top dress with compost. Once in a while, dig out the excess to keep it in check.

Lemongrass

Lemongrass is a tropical plant used liberally in Thai and other Asian cuisines for its lovely zingy, lemony flavour.

Although lemongrass is native to the tropics and is frost tender, it can be grown as an annual or a tender perennial in cold climates. Lemongrass will grow from root cuttings or can be propagated by dividing an existing plant, so, if you know someone who grows it, ask for a piece of stem with some root on it, or a small clump. (Wear gloves if you divide a lemongrass clump as the leaves have sharp edges.) Otherwise, buy small plants or start off as seed indoors. Plant outdoors in pots or borders, feed with lots of organic compost and water generously – lemongrass likes lots of water. Lemongrass will grow to around 1.2m (4 feet) tall and is an attractive ornamental.

In cold climates, cut back a little and bring indoors during winter. For cooking, peel away the tough outer leaves and use the pale bulbous section only, either crushed or finely sliced.

Bay Leaf (Sweet Bay or Laurel Tree)
Bay leaves are common in the cuisines of Asia and the Mediterranean, where the bay tree is thought to have originated, and an essential ingredient in a bouquet garni.

Most people know the bay leaf as a grey-green, hard dry leaf that comes in a little plastic bag and, more often than not, after using the odd one, the remainder are left languishing at the back of the pantry shelf. However, bay leaves can be used fresh and, as is usually the case in the wonderful world of herbs, fresh is better for flavour and aroma than the old, dried leaves commonly found in shops and supermarkets in the west.

The flavour of bay leaves is quite strong, and most dishes require only one or two leaves. It is, however, very satisfying to be able to pick one fresh off the tree when needed to add that distinctive robust flavour to all manner of savoury soups, casseroles, sauces and curries.

Bay trees are relatively easy to grow, particularly in warm climates where they can grow to 25m (60 feet) tall and look quite beautiful. In cooler climates bay trees will not grow anywhere near as tall. Grown in containers they make gorgeous patio plants and can be kept pruned to a relatively compact size. Container grown plants can easily be over wintered indoors in very cold climates.

When cooking with bay leaves, whether fresh or dried, use sparingly, tear them up before using to release the aromatic oils and remove them before serving the dish.

4

THAI FOOD AND
GOOD HEALTH

For those who love the tantalizingly lively and spicy flavours of Thai food, it is an added bonus that Thai cuisine is incredibly healthy, in fact possibly one of the healthiest you can eat. In eastern cultures it has been accepted for centuries that certain spices and herbs have the ability to prevent and even cure many ailments. It is usual within these cultures, even today, to treat many common illnesses with age old 'remedies' – everyday ingredients often residing in the pantry or growing in the garden.

Having been brought up in such a culture, it is 'normal' for me to use common ingredients as medicines for minor health issues. For example, I still reach for the fennel seeds and cardamom for stomach upsets; prepare a ginger 'tea' or soup for digestive problems or nausea and use turmeric both taken in food or drink and externally for strains and sprains. In recent years, as science has proved their worth, it has become more common in the west to use natural ingredients such as these to treat a range of conditions.

Many of the fresh herbs and spices, such as coriander, turmeric, galangal, lemongrass, mint and fresh chillies used in Thai cooking have proven immune boosting and disease fighting ability. Even coconut milk and cream, items perceived to be fattening and unhealthy, are in fact considered by nutritional experts and scientists to be extremely good for you. Including these ingredients in your diet will not only make your food taste great, but will also assist in promoting optimal health and well being.

Turmeric

Turmeric is a known anti-inflammatory. The active ingredient abundant in turmeric, curcumin, has been shown to be effective in relieving symptoms of arthritis, fighting infections and speeding wound healing. Turmeric is available in capsule form from leading healthfood stores and supermarkets but is comparatively expensive. Eating foods, such as curries, cooked with turmeric is a good, inexpensive way to get the health benefits of this useful spice.

Galangal

A relative of ginger and similar in appearance and flavour, galangal has been used for centuries in holistic medicine to treat a wide variety of ailments. Like ginger, galangal is very effective for alleviating abdominal discomfort, vomiting and nausea and aiding digestion. It is also effective in improving peripheral blood circulation and reducing the pain associated with arthritis. Try this 'tea' next time you have a stomach upset or feel nauseous – steep about a tablespoonful of grated ginger or galangal in a cup of boiling water for about ten minutes. Strain and sweeten with sugar or honey and drink while still warm.

Lemongrass

Lemongrass is used extensively in Thai cooking and ancient Chinese medicine. It has been shown to be particularly useful for reducing the incidence of colds and flu and relieving symptoms such as fever and headache.

Coriander Seed

Coriander seed has been used for centuries by healers all over the world, including the UK, Greece, China and India, to treat gastrointestinal problems such as flatulence and bloating, bacterial and fungal infections and to stimulate appetite.

Chillies

Researchers in Thailand first noticed that people who ate large amounts of chilli experienced a lower incidence of potentially dangerous blood clots. After studying data from other countries where hot and spicy food is commonly consumed by the general population, scientists concluded that the active ingredient – capsaicin – found in chillies does indeed possess the ability to break down blood clots. Applied topically in an ointment, capsaicin has also been found to control the chronic pain associated with conditions such as shingles and neuralgia. Capsaicin ointments are now available on prescription.

Mint

Mint has long been integral to the cuisine and medicinal practices of Indian, European and Middle Eastern societies. It is well known for its ability to soothe the digestive tract, reduce the severity of stomach ache and alleviate the discomfort of irritable bowel syndrome (IBS). Mint also has documented anti-fungal properties, and animal studies show that it can prevent the formation of lung, skin and colon cancers. Mint supplements and teas are readily available, or try making this delicious fresh mint tea: steep a small handful of fresh mint leaves and a teaspoon (or teabag) of black or green tea in hot (not boiling) water for about five minutes. Keep covered to prevent the volatile oils from escaping. Strain and sweeten with honey or sugar if desired.

Basil

Basil is a lovely, robustly aromatic herb used widely in Thai, Indian, Italian, Mediterranean and other cuisines. Rich in flavonoids, basil has been shown to prevent cell damage from radiation and free radicals. Also, the numerous volatile oils in basil have demonstrated bactericidal activity and been shown to be effective against organisms that have become resistant to antibiotics. A solution containing just 1 per cent of these oils can be used to rinse vegetables and kill infectious bacteria that cause diarrhoea. Some dieticians recommend adding basil to salad dressings to ensure safety when eating salads.

Basil also exhibits anti-inflammatory properties, apparently in a similar manner to aspirin, making it a good herb to consume by people who suffer with arthritis.

Coconut Milk and Cream

Coconut milk and particularly coconut cream are generally perceived to be high in calories and to be contributing to obesity and related illnesses. Yes, it is a calorie dense food but that is a plus in many countries. Yes, it does contain fat, but the fats in coconut milk and cream are considered by experts to be the good fats, not the bad disease-causing ones. The principal fatty acid in coconut is lauric acid, the same fatty acid found in abundance in mother's milk. Lauric acid strengthens the immune system and protects bone and brain tissue.

It is now known that eating good fat is essential to good health and even to weight control. The fats in coconut have been shown to lower bad cholesterol (LDL) and raise good cholesterol (HDL), boost immunity, modulate insulin levels and provide valuable fatty acids often lacking in western diets. It is thought that the fats in coconut milk and coconut cream do not cause weight gain as readily as polyunsaturated fats.

5

EQUIPMENT AND COOKING BASICS

It never ceases to amaze me how something as delicious as Thai food can be so simple, flexible, undemanding and so quick to cook. All you have to do is equip yourself with a few simple kitchen items, get to know a few basic principles and techniques, and you can prepare the most wonderful Thai dishes in minutes.

Equipment

The typical Thai kitchen takes quite a simple approach to kitchen equipment so you really don't need any special items to cook great Thai food. Many Thais have very minimalist cooking facilities with few kitchen utensils, yet the elaborate and diverse food they cook is simply amazing – grinding spices and making rich and colourful curry pastes with nothing more than a sharp knife and a pestle and mortar and cooking a range of mouthwatering dishes with one or two small pots and a single wok. Furthermore, simple, portable kitchens set up by the roadside cook and sell incredibly delicious food to hundreds of people daily without much ado.

Most of us in the west are not quite that adept however, so below are some kitchen items that will make preparing and cooking Thai food really easy and quick for the western cook.

- A small blender for making curry pastes
- A coffee grinder for grinding spices
- A well seasoned wok for stir-fries and Pad Thai

If you don't have a blender or coffee grinder and don't wish to purchase these items, you can use a pestle and mortar for both grinding spices and making pastes – this is the traditional way and you will produce great curry pastes, but it is more laborious.

If you don't own a wok and don't want to get one, you can use a deep frying pan or saucepan. However, I will explain a bit about why a wok does what it does so you can decide whether to get one or use an existing utensil that may help you do much the same thing. In contrast to the favoured pots and pans of western cooks that allow for long, slow, even cooking, a wok is designed to be lightning fast. It will heat up rapidly and cool down just as fast. The thin metal of a good wok will transfer most of the heat of the flame to the food inside it almost immediately, cooking and searing the food at super speed whilst maintaining its freshness and crunch and giving it the caramelization that is characteristic of a good Thai dish. This speed of cooking is particularly important for Pad Thai and stir-fries.

Fortunately, a good wok need not be expensive. In fact, you can buy the cheapest and thinnest you can find, with two provisos: it is better not to buy an aluminium wok or one with a non-stick coating. Aluminium doesn't heat up quickly and common coating materials don't tolerate high temperatures and are likely to chip and flake and give off toxic fumes when heated to the temperatures you will need for Thai cooking. Unless you wish to spend more, look for a thin carbon steel wok about 34 cm (14 inches) wide. If you use gas to cook, buy a round-bottomed wok that comes with a ring for setting the wok on. This shape allows the flames to travel up the sides of the wok for better heat distribution.

The secret is in the 'seasoning' – of the wok that is.

How to Season Your Wok

A well seasoned wok will prevent food from sticking to it and will be protected from rusting. You can buy ready seasoned woks at a price. Otherwise, there are varying ways of seasoning a wok but all use oil, salt and heat to do the job and I find this one easy and effective.

- Spray a generous amount of cooking oil over the cooking surface of the wok, or pour about a quarter of a cup of oil into it and spread it over the surface using a paper towel. Discard any excess oil that pools at the bottom. You don't need to use expensive oil, any cooking oil will do.

- Place the wok on medium-high heat and heat it for about 5 minutes. Make sure the extractor fan is on and windows are open as the wok will get very hot and the oil will smoke.

- Turn off the heat and add about half a cup of table or cooking salt to the hot pan. Take a thick wad of paper towels or a kitchen rag and rub the salt well into the wok. Take care as it will be quite hot.

- Discard excess salt and place the wok on medium-high heat again. Heat again for a further 4–5 minutes.

- Turn off the heat, allow the wok to cool and wipe clean with a damp cloth. Spray or rub a little more oil onto the surface. Your previously shiny wok should now be blackened, seasoned and ready to cook up a feast.

This process can be repeated whenever your wok ceases to be non-stick.

Other Basics

Cooking Thai food is amazingly simple and speedy once you learn the basics. These few basic principles of Thai cooking once put into practice will have you cooking delicious Thai food in minutes.

- Stock your pantry with all the non-perishable items that you plan to use regularly. Ingredients like coconut milk, fish sauce, soy sauce, palm sugar, dried shrimp, rice noodles and jasmine rice all keep well.

- Have your basic equipment at the ready and your wok seasoned if you plan to use a wok.

- Consider growing herbs that you will use regularly so that they are always on hand.

6

THAI COOKING TECHNIQUES, SECRETS AND TIPS

The Secret is in the Preparation

The secret to cooking great Thai food successfully is in the preparation. This is particularly true for wok cooking when the cooking itself is fast and furious. The following tips will help to make your Thai cooking really good, easy and incredibly quick.

- Prepare your curry pastes ahead of time. Fresh curry paste will keep in the fridge for up to a week, but can also be frozen for up to six months. Once you have a good paste to hand, the rest is easy.

- If you buy ready made pastes – and there are some reasonably good ones about – the following tip will help you bring your purchased paste up to scratch. Note the list of ingredients on the label and supplement the paste with fresh ingredients and anything else that is not included. Most commercially made pastes are deficient or lacking in several important ingredients such as lime, coriander root and ground spices. At the very least I add extra garlic, coriander root or stems and lime rind if I use a ready made paste.

- Prepare and bottle quantities of Pad Thai and other sauces that you plan to use regularly. This is simply a matter of mixing together ingredients such as soy sauce, fish sauce, tamarind and other ready prepared sauces or ground spices so that you are not reaching for several jars and bottles once you start cooking.

- Roast, grind and store spices in small quantities ready for use.

- Use good quality, heat tolerant oils for your Thai dishes. Many Thai chefs use organic coconut or peanut oil but other good oils are sunflower, corn and rice bran. Non-GM canola is also good if you can get it.

Before You Start Cooking

- Chop all vegetables and herbs and place them in separate mounds on a tray or large plate (or separate dishes if you don't mind the washing up) in the order that they are to be used.

- Slice meat, fish, tofu or chicken ready for use. Refrigerate if not using immediately but remove from the fridge 30 minutes or so before they are needed to bring to room temperature. This ensures that the maximum cooking temperature is maintained during cooking.

- Combine all the sauces and seasonings that you will need in a cup ready for use. That way you won't be reaching for one bottle after another and will be far less likely to miss something. Thai cooks, especially the vendors of delicious street food, have large quantities of their regularly used sauces and spices mixed and ready to use.

- Have wooden spoons, tongs or any other equipment that you will need at the ready, including all serving dishes and utensils.

- When cooking stir-fries or noodle dishes make sure your wok or pan is really hot before starting to cook.

Finding the Sweet, Sour, Salty, Spicy Flavour Balance

Balancing and harmonizing the four key flavours is the secret to obtaining those wonderful flavours characteristic of Thai food. The intensity of flavour is very much a matter of personal preference and you can use larger or smaller amounts of the four ingredients depending on how intense you want the overall flavour to be, but no one flavour should over-power another. Just as you might vary the amount of chilli, garlic or ginger in Indian dishes according to the taste and tolerance of the diner, you can vary the amount of the key flavouring ingredients in Thai dishes so that the intensity of flavour feels right to you. However, Thai food should never taste dull and there should be enough of each of the four flavours to create a lively symphony of flavour on your tastebuds.

It is also important to be aware that recipes for Thai dishes are, to some extent, guides only, because flavours of many ingredients such as fish sauce, limes and lemongrass will vary according to the season, where they come from and how old they are. Taste testing, therefore, is absolutely essential. Flavours of fish and soy sauce also vary from one brand to another so finding a brand that you like and sticking to it will help give you some consistency.

Extra fish sauce, soy sauce, sliced chilli and lime wedges should be served with the meal, much like salt and pepper, to cater for individual tastes.

Tips for Taste Testing and Balancing
- Too spicy hot. Add more fish sauce and lime juice to counter the heat and balance with a little sugar.

- Too salty. Add lime juice, lemon juice or tamarind paste dissolved in a little water and balance with a touch of sugar.

- Too sour. Add palm sugar or any sugar you have and balance with a little fish or soy sauce.

- Not spicy enough. Add fresh chillies, chilli powder, cayenne, ground pepper or chilli sauce.

- Not salty enough. Add fish sauce or soy sauce in preference to salt for a better depth of flavour.

- Not sour enough. Add lime or lemon juice or tamarind paste dissolved in a little water. Balance with some sugar if needed.

- Remember you can always add some coconut milk or cream to tone down the flavours too.

Experiment by making some sauce with a little stock or coconut milk and adding chilli, garlic, fish sauce, lime juice and sugar one at a time, tasting the sauce before adding the next key ingredient to experience the impact of each on the overall flavour.

Tips for Great Stir-Frying

Prior preparation is the holy grail of great stir-frying, followed very closely by a really hot, well seasoned wok or frying pan. Stir-fries are cooked at high heat and super speed, a method of cooking that makes the food taste fresh and delicious and keeps the nutrients intact.

- Prepare everything you need as outlined in Before You Start Cooking section, page 33. There will be no time to start looking for this bottle or that piece of equipment once you start cooking.

- Start with a really hot wok which is well coated with oil, right up to about 2.5 cm (1 inch) of the rim.

- Cooking at high heat requires very little oil but if the wok gets too dry add a little stock, wine or water rather than more oil so that your food is not greasy.

- For the best stir-fried vegetables, slice thinner those that take longer to cook than those that cook quickly. For example, carrots should be sliced thinly whilst snow peas (mangetout) should be left whole. Cook vegetables only briefly until the colours brighten. They should be crisp and bright so it is important not to over cook them.

- For perfect stir-fried rice, use pre-cooked rice that is no more than a day old. Spread the rice onto a large plate or tray, spray or sprinkle with a little oil and gently work it through with your fingers until all the grains are coated. You will get beautifully fluffy results and no sticky clumps.

7

THAI CURRY PASTES

Thai curry pastes are a mix of aromatic fresh herbs, chillies and spices that combine to create an explosion of intense, complex and delicious flavours. These pastes are the basis of all types of Thai curries, many stir-fries and some noodle dishes. Each paste has different characteristics and colouring and its own unique taste, even though many of the primary ingredients are the same. Seemingly minor changes to the basic ingredients and the method of preparation produce an array of different colours and varied and delicious flavours.

Curry pastes keep well in the fridge for up to a week and can be frozen for six months, so by preparing some when you have time you can make delicious Thai curries in minutes whenever you wish. If you decide to freeze your home-made curry paste, a useful tip is to divide it into one tablespoon portions so that you can take out just as much as you need. Ice-cube trays are great for this purpose.

Red Curry Paste is a hot paste, the red colouring being derived entirely from hot, dried red chillies. It is a versatile paste used to flavour a range of curries, soups and stir-fries.

Green Curry Paste is thought to be (in Thailand) the hottest of all Thai curry pastes, its green colouring coming from fresh herbs and a generous quantity of hot green chillies. You can use the larger, milder chillies if you don't want so much heat. Green curry is perhaps the most unique to Thailand as it is very different from the curries of other countries. This paste is used exclusively for green Thai curries.

Yellow Curry Paste has a mellow spicy-sweet flavour and produces curry that is similar in colour and taste to Indian curries. The yellow colour is due to the use of turmeric. This mild paste is used with or without coconut milk and is traditionally used to make chicken and potato or fish curries.

Panang Curry Paste is based on red curry paste but contains more Indian style spices. Panang curry is traditionally cooked with meat only – no vegetables are used – and with just enough coconut milk to cover. The resulting curry is quite dry, unlike red or green curry which has much more sauce, but is very flavoursome.

Massaman Curry Paste is based largely on dried spices not typical of Thai cuisine. Its origins are in the deep south of Thailand on the border of Malaysia so it is significantly influenced by the local Malaysian cuisine. Beef or lamb is the traditional meat for this curry but it is also good with chicken. Massaman curry is very aromatic but comparatively mild as the heat is mellowed by the coconut cream, onions and potatoes.

Jazzing up Shop Bought Pastes

Home-made curry pastes are hard to beat for flavour and aroma but you can buy ready made pastes from Asian grocers and supermarkets. If you choose to buy a commercially made curry paste, note the list of ingredients on the label and add whatever is missing in the ready made preparation when you use it. I also add some fresh ingredients like extra garlic, coriander root and lime peel as the wonderful aromas and flavours of these ingredients are generally minimal in these pastes.

Other Pastes and Sauces

There are several tasty Thai pastes and sauces used as flavourings or dipping sauces. Below are some of the most popular.

Roast Chilli Paste *nahm prik pow*, or 'roasted chilli paste', is not a curry paste but a flavouring agent commonly used in Thai cooking. It is used to flavour soups, stir-fries and noodle dishes and is also fantastic as a dipping sauce or as an addition to dressings for Thai salads. As the name implies, the main ingredient is dried red chillies roasted over hot charcoal until a deep, dark red. Against the smoky, fragrant base of pungent roasted flavours the paste bursts with a complex mix of sweet, salty, spicy and tangy flavours that complement a range of Thai dishes.

Peanut Sauce is a firm favourite in Thailand, and, unlike most western recipes which use commercially prepared peanut butter, it is made with freshly roasted peanuts ground and combined with other tasty ingredients. And you can taste the difference. It is used not just for making satays but also as a tasty dipping sauce for meat, seafood and vegetables.

Pad Thai Sauce is a delicious and potent mix of tangy, spicy and sweet flavours. A good sauce is essential for making great Pad Thai.

Thai Sweet Chilli Sauce has a distinctive flavour and is excellent as a dip for lots of different dishes.

8

WEIGHTS AND MEASURES

Both metric and imperial measurements have been given in this book with the imperial measures being rounded up or down to the nearest unit. Remember to use one or the other and not to combine imperial and metric measurements in one recipe.

All spoon measurements throughout the book are **slightly rounded** spoonfuls unless specified as being level.

Fluid ounces refer to the British fluid ounce which is slightly smaller than the US equivalent. This difference is not significant for the recipes in this book.

Cup size is the metric cup (250 ml) or half a US pint.

Some conversions are given in the table below:

Measure	UK	USA	Australia
Teaspoon	5 ml	4.93 ml	5 ml
Dessertspoon	10 ml	–	10 ml
Tablespoon	15 ml	14.79 ml	20 ml
Cup	285 ml	236.59 ml	250 ml (metric up)
Fluid oz	28.41 ml	29.57 ml	–
1 litre	2.2 pints	2.1 pints	

9

STEP-BY-STEP RECIPES

THAI CURRY PASTES

OTHER PASTES AND SAUCES

MASSAMAN CURRY PASTE

This combines Indian and Thai flavours to produce a robust and delicious curry that is aromatic and spicy without a lot of heat. Add extra chilli if you like.

Makes about 12 tablespoons of paste
Preparation time: 20–25 minutes

12 dried red chillies or more to taste
12 cloves garlic, peeled
4 shallots or 1 medium onion, sliced
1 tsp sliced lemongrass, white part only, chopped
1 tbsp grated galangal
1 tsp grated kaffir lime rind or lime zest
1 tbsp scraped, sliced coriander roots
1 tsp sea salt
2 tbsp oil
1 tbsp ground coriander
1 tsp ground cumin
1 tsp ground pepper
1 tsp shrimp paste

- Soak the chillies in hot water for a few minutes until soft. Remove the seeds and set aside. Be careful when handling the chillies (see page 44).

- Combine all the ingredients except the ground spices and shrimp paste in the bowl of a food processor, add a tablespoon of water and process until smooth. Or pound in a pestle and mortar until you have a smooth paste.

- Add the ground spices and shrimp paste and process until well combined.

- Transfer the paste to a clean jar and refrigerate for up to a week or divide into 1 tablespoon portions and freeze in ice-cube trays or other suitable containers.

Tip: *If you are going to keep the paste in the fridge for any length of time, pour just enough oil over the top of it to cover. This will help keep the paste fresh.*

RED CURRY PASTE

This rich red paste is the most versatile of all Thai curry pastes and is used in a wide range of dishes. It is typically very hot but you can reduce the heat by using fewer of the small Thai hot chillies or substituting with long mild red chillies in order to achieve the red colour without the heat.

If you are making this paste using a pestle and mortar, using coarse sea salt helps to grind all the ingredients down.

Note: Be careful when handling chillies as they will irritate the skin and eyes. Wear thin rubber gloves and be careful not to touch your eyes. Or wash your hands thoroughly afterwards.

Makes about 12 tablespoons of paste
Preparation time: 20–25 minutes

16 small dried red chillies
1 tbsp coriander seeds
2 tsp cumin seeds
2 tsp white or black peppercorns
3 French shallots or 1 small onion, sliced
1 tbsp grated galangal or ginger
12 cloves garlic, peeled
2 tbsp sliced fresh or frozen lemongrass – white part only
3 tsp grated kaffir lime rind or lime zest
1 tbsp scraped, sliced coriander roots and stems
1 tsp shrimp paste
1 tsp sea salt

- Soak the chillies in hot water for about 10 minutes, drain and remove the seeds.

- Dry roast the coriander, cumin and peppercorns in a small hot pan, stirring and shaking the pan constantly to ensure they don't burn, for about a minute or until fragrant. Transfer immediately to a plate lined with kitchen paper and cool.

- Grind the spices to a fine powder in a mortar and pestle or electric coffee grinder.

- Combine all the ingredients except the ground spices in the bowl of a food processor, add a tablespoon of water and process until smooth. Or pound in a pestle and mortar until you have a smooth paste.

- Stir in the ground spices. Transfer the paste to a clean jar and refrigerate for up to a week or divide into 1 tablespoon portions and freeze in ice-cube trays or other suitable containers.

Tip: *If you are going to keep the paste in the fridge for any length of time, pour just enough oil over the top of it to cover. This will help keep the paste fresh.*

GREEN CURRY PASTE

This authentic recipe produces a hot, aromatic paste that can be used for all Thai green curries. If you are making this paste using a pestle and mortar, use coarse sea salt as this helps to grind all the ingredients down.

Makes about 12 tablespoons of paste
Preparation time: 20–25 minutes

2 tsp coriander seeds
1 tsp cumin seeds
2 tsp white peppercorns
20 fresh green Thai chillies or a combination of mild
   and hot chillies
10 cloves garlic, peeled
3 French shallots, sliced
1 tbsp grated galangal
1 tbsp sliced fresh or frozen lemongrass, white part only
2 tbsp sliced kaffir lime rind or lime zest
1 tbsp scraped, sliced coriander roots and stems
1 tsp shrimp paste
1 tsp sea salt

- Combine the coriander, cumin seeds and peppercorns in a small pan and roast over medium heat, stirring constantly, for a minute or two until aromatic. Immediately transfer to a plate lined with kitchen paper and cool.

- Grind the spices using an electric coffee grinder or pound in a pestle and mortar until finely ground.

- Combine all the ingredients except for the ground spices in the bowl of a food processor, add a tablespoon of water and process until smooth. Or pound in a pestle and mortar until you have a smooth paste.

- Stir in the ground spices. Transfer the paste to a clean jar and refrigerate for up to a week or divide into 1 tablespoon portions and freeze in ice-cube trays or other suitable containers.

Tip: *If you are going to keep the paste in the fridge for any length of time, pour just enough oil over the top of it to cover. This will help keep the paste fresh.*

YELLOW CURRY PASTE

This is a flavoursome paste with mild flavours – ideal for anyone who likes spicy food without the heat.

    Note: Be careful when handling chillies as they will irritate the skin and eyes. Wear thin rubber gloves and be careful not to touch your eyes. Or wash your hands thoroughly afterwards.

Makes about 10 tablespoons of paste
Preparation time: 20–25 minutes

6 dried red chillies
1 tbsp coriander seeds
2 tsp cumin seeds
1 tsp black peppercorns
1 tsp black mustard seeds
2.5 cm (1 inch) stick cinnamon
2 tbsp oil
4 shallots or one medium onion, sliced
12 cloves garlic, peeled and sliced
2 tsp grated galangal or ginger
1 tbsp sliced fresh or frozen lemongrass, white part only
2 kaffir lime leaves, sliced (or 1 tsp lime zest)
1 tsp sea salt
2 tsp turmeric
1 tsp shrimp paste

- Soak the chillies in hot water for a few minutes until soft. Remove the seeds and set aside.

- Meanwhile, place the coriander, cumin, peppercorns, mustard seeds and cinnamon stick in a small pan and roast over medium heat for a minute or two, stirring constantly until aromatic. Transfer immediately to a plate lined with kitchen paper and cool.

- Grind the spices using an electric coffee grinder or pound in a pestle and mortar until finely ground. Set aside.

- Heat the oil in a small pan over medium heat until just hot and add the chopped shallots (or onion), garlic, galangal or ginger. Stir-fry for about 3 minutes over gentle heat until soft. Cool.

- Combine all the ingredients except the ground spices, turmeric and shrimp paste in the bowl of a food processor, add a tablespoon of water and process until smooth. Or pound in a pestle and mortar until you have a smooth paste.

- Add the spice mixture, turmeric and shrimp paste and process until well combined.

- Transfer the paste to a clean jar and refrigerate for up to a week or divide into 1 tablespoon portions and freeze in ice-cube trays or other suitable containers.

Tip: *If you are going to keep the paste in the fridge for any length of time, pour just enough oil over the top of it to cover. This will help keep the paste fresh.*

PANANG CURRY PASTE

The dried spices and milder chillies in this recipe impart rich spicy flavours without the heat of red curry paste. It is ideal for thicker textured curries such as the popular Panang Beef Curry.

Note: Be careful when handling chillies as they will irritate the skin and eyes. See page 48.

Makes about 12 tablespoons of paste
Preparation time: 20–25 minutes

5 long dried red chillies
1 tsp coriander seeds
½ tsp cumin seeds
1 tsp whole white peppercorns
2 cloves
1 cm (½ inch) piece of cinnamon
5 shallots or 1 large onion, sliced
10 cloves garlic, peeled
2 tsp grated galangal
2 tsp sliced fresh or frozen lemongrass, white part only
1 tbsp scraped, sliced coriander roots and stems
1 tbsp grated kaffir lime rind or lime zest
1 tbsp soft brown sugar
1 tsp sea salt
2 tsp shrimp paste

- Grind the chillies and spices to a fine powder using a coffee grinder or pestle and mortar. Set aside.

- Combine all the ingredients in the bowl of a food processor, add a tablespoon of water and process until smooth. Or pound in a pestle and mortar until you have a smooth paste.

- Transfer the paste to a clean jar and refrigerate for up to a week or divide into 1 tablespoon portions and freeze in ice-cube trays or other suitable containers.

Tip: *If you are going to keep the paste in the fridge for any length of time, pour just enough oil over the top of it to cover. This will help keep the paste fresh.*

THAI PEANUT SAUCE

This is a spectacularly delicious sauce that is much too good to keep just for satays. Savour it as a dip with fresh crunchy vegetables or enjoy it stirred into leftover noodles as a quick and tasty snack. As a bonus, it is really easy to make.

Makes about 1 cup
Preparation time: 5 minutes

1 cup dry roasted peanuts, roughly chopped
1 clove garlic, minced
2 tsp sesame oil
2 tbsp grated palm or soft brown sugar
2 tbsp fish or soy sauce
1 tsp tamarind paste
1 tsp chilli powder or hot chilli sauce
4 tbsp coconut milk
4 tbsp water

- Combine all the ingredients in a blender jug and blend until perfectly smooth. Thin the sauce with a little more coconut milk until you have the desired consistency.

- If not using immediately, transfer to a clean jar and store in the fridge for up to two weeks.

ROAST CHILLI PASTE

This rustic paste (*nahm prik pao*) with its deeply intense, smoky flavour is very popular with Thais. It is incredibly tasty and aromatic and very versatile. The secret to making an authentic, flavoursome paste is to roast the ingredients until they are nicely charred and powerfully aromatic but not burnt.

Note: Be careful when handling chillies as they will irritate the skin and eyes. Wear thin rubber gloves and be careful not to touch your eyes. Or wash your hands thoroughly afterwards. Use an extractor fan or open the windows when roasting.

Makes just over a cup
Preparation and cooking time: 45 minutes

1 cup small dried red chillies, de-seeded
6 shallots or 2 small onions, roughly chopped
12 cloves garlic, peeled and roughly chopped
½ cup oil
4 tbsp grated palm or soft brown sugar
2 tbsp tamarind paste dissolved in 2 tbsp warm water
1 tbsp soy sauce
1 tbsp fish sauce
1 tbsp shrimp paste

- Heat a wok or frying pan over low to medium heat and roast the chillies, stirring and shaking the pan constantly, until aromatic and dark, about 4–5 minutes. Remove from the heat and transfer to a plate lined with kitchen paper. Set aside to cool.

- Increase the heat slightly and dry fry the shallots (or onions) and garlic until soft and slightly charred, about 5 minutes. Remove from the heat and transfer to another plate. Set aside to cool.

- Place the roasted ingredients in the bowl of a food processor and process until finely chopped. Add about half the oil and process to a smooth paste.

- Heat the remaining oil in a wok or heavy based frying pan and add the paste. The oil needs to be hot enough so that the paste sizzles immediately.

- Stir-fry the paste over medium heat for about 5 minutes or until it darkens and releases the oil. Set aside to cool.

- Add all the remaining ingredients and stir into the paste until completely incorporated.

- Transfer the paste to a clean jar with a tight fitting lid and store in the fridge for up to a month. The oil will rise to the surface of the paste. Stir this in each time before using.

PAD THAI SAUCE

This flavour packed sauce will help you make the best tasting Pad Thai ever. It is made with intensely flavoursome ingredients and tastes quite strong on its own but the flavours balance out wonderfully when used with the noodles and other ingredients that go to make Pad Thai.

Makes about 1½ cups – enough for 4–6 Pad Thai servings
Preparation time: 5 minutes

2 tbsp tamarind paste
5 tbsp grated palm or soft brown sugar
½ cup hot water
6 tbsp fish sauce
2–3 tsp chilli powder

- Dissolve the tamarind paste and sugar in the hot water. Add the remaining ingredients and mix to combine.

- Do the taste test and if the sauce tastes too sweet add a little more tamarind paste and fish sauce. If it's not sweet enough, add a little more sugar. Although strong, it should have a nice balance of salty, sweet and hot flavours.

- Transfer the sauce to a clean jar and keep refrigerated for up to a week.

THAI SWEET CHILLI SAUCE

This hot, sweet, sticky sauce is so much tastier than the bottled variety and is well worth making. This recipe produces a medium hot sauce but you can make it as mild or as hot as you like by varying the quantity and type of chillies.

Note: Be careful when handling chillies as they will irritate the skin and eyes. Wear thin rubber gloves and be careful not to touch your eyes. Or wash your hands thoroughly afterwards.

Makes about 1 cup
Preparation and cooking time: 30 minutes

6 hot red chillies, roughly chopped
8 cloves garlic, roughly chopped
1 cup white sugar
1 cup white vinegar
1 tbsp fish sauce
1 tbsp lime juice

- Combine the chillies and garlic in the bowl of a food processor and process until finely chopped.

- Place the chilli and garlic mixture, sugar and vinegar in a small saucepan and stir over low heat until the sugar is dissolved.

- Bring to the boil and simmer for about 15 minutes until the sauce is a syrupy consistency.

- Stir in the fish sauce and lime juice. Transfer the hot sauce to a sterilized jar with a tight fitting lid. Store in the fridge once opened.

APPETIZERS AND SNACKS

Good dining western style dictates that the meal consists of at least three courses – a starter, main course and dessert. In Thailand, as in most Asian countries, there is no such thing as a starter and a range of different types of dishes are served at once, with everyone helping themselves to a little of everything. Thais are, however, enthusiastic 'snackers' and there are hundreds of fragrant, colourful and tasty titbits and snacks that make excellent appetizers and starters. Here are just a few quick and easy recipes.

THAI FISH CAKES

These deliciously spicy fish cakes are very different in taste and texture from the western version. A popular Thai dish, it is extremely easy to prepare and makes a great starter or snack.

Note: Be careful when handling the chilli (see page 58).

Serves 4–6
Preparation and cooking time: 40 minutes

500 g (1 lb) white fish fillets, sliced into chunks
2 tbsp red curry paste (page 44)
½ cup green beans, finely sliced
4 kaffir lime leaves, finely sliced (or 1 tsp lime zest)
1 red chilli, finely sliced
2 tsp soft brown sugar
1 tbsp fish sauce
1 egg, lightly beaten

Oil for deep frying

To serve: Sweet and Sour Cucumber Sauce – Combine ½ cup each of sugar and vinegar in a small saucepan and stir over low heat until sugar dissolves. Cool and add ½ cup of finely diced cucumber, 2 finely sliced spring onions including the green shoots and 1 tbsp chopped peanuts.

- Process the fish pieces to a paste using a food processor, or pound in a pestle and mortar. Transfer to a large mixing bowl and add all the remaining ingredients. Mix thoroughly until well combined.

- Take about a heaped tablespoon of the mixture, and using damp hands form into a patty just over 1 cm (½ inch) thick. Repeat with the remaining mixture.

- Deep fry in batches in hot oil for about 3 minutes, turning once, until cooked through. Drain on two layers of kitchen paper and serve hot.

THAI LETTUCE WRAPS

The combination of cool, crispy lettuce and the warm, tasty filling is an absolute delight for adults and children alike. Make them with chicken, pork, seafood or tofu or even a combination of two or more of these fillings. Leave the chilli out and serve it separately if you are cooking for young children.

Note: Be careful when handling the chilli as it will irritate the skin and eyes. Wear thin rubber gloves and be careful not to touch your eyes. Or wash your hands thoroughly afterwards.

Serves 4
Preparation and cooking time: 30–40 minutes

Sauce: In a small bowl or cup combine 2 tbsp each of lime juice, soy sauce, fish sauce and ½ cup of plum sauce.

1 fresh iceberg lettuce
2 tbsp oil
2 shallots or 1 small onion, finely sliced
1 tbsp fresh ginger, grated
4 cloves garlic, finely chopped
1 red chilli, de-seeded and finely chopped
500 g (1 lb) minced chicken (or meat/seafood/tofu)
½ cup shredded red or green cabbage
½ cup grated carrot
3 spring onions, sliced at an angle into matchstick size pieces
1 cup bean sprouts
1 cup basil leaves
½ cup roasted peanuts, roughly chopped (optional)

To serve: fish sauce, soy sauce, Thai chilli sauce, lime wedges

- Slice the stem off the lettuce and separate the leaves. Rinse and drain. Place in the crisper section of fridge.

- Heat a wok or frying pan on medium heat and add the oil. Swirl to coat, add the shallots (or onion), ginger, garlic and chilli and stir-fry on medium heat for one minute or until fragrant.

- Add the chicken (or meat/seafood/tofu) and stir-fry on medium to high heat for two minutes.

- Add the cabbage, carrot and spring onions and stir-fry for about a minute. Continue stir-frying and drizzle in the sauce. Stir-fry for another minute or so until everything is coated with the sauce and any liquid has evaporated.

- Stir in the bean sprouts and stir-fry until mixed. Remove from the heat and do the taste test. Stir in a little fish sauce or lime juice if desired.

- Transfer to a serving dish and serve with the lettuce leaves and let everyone help themselves.

- To make the wraps, place a tablespoon or so of filling onto a lettuce leaf, top with a few basil leaves, a sprinkling of peanuts and additional sauces. Wrap up and enjoy.

THAI CHICKEN SATAY

This Thai satay with succulent chicken pieces smothered in a delicious home-made peanut sauce is a real treat. Serve it as a side dish, as finger food or as a tasty starter. You can make it with strips of pork or beef for a change.

If using wooden skewers soak in cold water for about 20 minutes so that they don't burn during cooking.

Serves 4
Preparation and cooking time: 45–50 minutes
(plus marinating time)

Marinade
3 tbsp finely sliced fresh or frozen lemongrass, white part only
3 shallots or 1 small onion, roughly chopped
2 cloves garlic
2.5 cm (1 inch) piece galangal or ginger, peeled and sliced
2 tsp ground coriander
1 tsp ground cumin
1 tsp ground black pepper
1 tsp turmeric
4 tbsp light soy sauce
4 tbsp fish sauce
4 tbsp palm or soft brown sugar
1 tbsp fresh lime juice
2 tsp grated lime zest

8 chicken thigh fillets, trimmed and sliced into strips
1 cup peanut sauce (page 51)

- Place all the marinade ingredients in the bowl of a food processor and process until finely chopped.

- Transfer the marinade into a bowl and add the chicken. Mix well, cover and refrigerate for at least 2 hours or overnight. Remove from the fridge about 30 minutes before cooking to allow the chicken to return to room temperature.

- Slide the strips of meat onto the bottom half of the skewer so that you can use the top part for turning and eating.

- Barbecue or grill the skewers for about 10–15 minutes, turning frequently, until the chicken is cooked through.

- Meanwhile, warm the peanut sauce, thinning with a little water or coconut milk if it is too thick.

- Brush the cooked chicken with the peanut sauce. Serve with the remaining peanut sauce and steamed rice.

THAI TEMPURA

These piping hot, deliciously crunchy morsels are easy to make and will have everyone asking for more. My family usually devour them quicker than I can cook them.

The fizzy water helps make the batter really light and crispy but you can use tap water instead. You can also substitute the chicken with finely diced tofu for a vegetarian version.

Note: Be careful when handling the chilli as it will irritate the skin and eyes. Wear thin rubber gloves and be careful not to touch your eyes. Or wash your hands thoroughly afterwards.

Serves 4
Preparation and cooking time: 25 minutes

Tempura Batter
½ cup plain flour
½ cup tapioca flour
½ cup cornflour
2 tsp baking powder
1 cup fizzy water (or cold tap water)
1 tbsp fish sauce

250 g (½ lb) chicken tenderloins, chopped into very
   small pieces
1 cup bean sprouts
3 spring onions, including green shoots, sliced
½ cup coriander, leaves and stems, chopped
1 red chilli, de-seeded and finely sliced
1 red or green capsicum, de-seeded and chopped
   into small dice

Oil for deep frying

To serve: Thai sweet chilli sauce (page 55)

- For the batter, combine the dry ingredients in a bowl and stir in the water and fish sauce until just combined. Don't over mix, a few small lumps won't matter. Add the remaining ingredients and gently stir into the batter.

- Heat the oil until a teaspoon of batter dropped into it sizzles and immediately rises to the top.

- Drop dessert spoonfuls of the mixture into the hot oil, being careful not to overcrowd the wok or pan.

- When the tempura browns at the edges, turn and fry the other side for a minute or so or until both sides are golden.

- Drain on kitchen paper and repeat with the remaining mixture. Serve piping hot.

VEGETARIAN FRESH SPRING ROLLS

A no-cook, tasty and healthy snack, starter or addition to a Thai meal, these spring rolls are full of fresh crunchy vegetables and fragrant herbs that are bursting with delicious Thai flavours. As always, the freshest tastiest vegetables will produce the best results.

Rice paper rounds are available in the Asian foods section of most supermarkets.

Makes 16
Preparation time: 35 minutes

Dressing: In a small bowl or cup combine 1 tbsp each of lime juice, soy sauce and fish sauce. Add 1 tsp grated palm or soft brown sugar and stir to dissolve.

90 g (3 oz) rice vermicelli noodles
1 carrot, grated or julienned
½ cup shredded cabbage
1 cup bean sprouts
1 red capsicum, sliced into thin strips
3 spring onions, thinly sliced
½ cup coriander leaves, chopped
½ cup Thai holy basil, shredded
16 rice paper rounds

To serve: Hoisin sauce, Thai sweet chilli sauce (page 55), peanut sauce (page 51) or dipping sauce of choice

- Soak the noodles in hot water for 10 minutes or as instructed on the packet. Drain, rinse with cold water and drain well. Using kitchen scissors, cut the noodles into short lengths.

- Combine all the ingredients except the rice paper in a bowl, add the dressing and mix well.

- Fill a large bowl with hand hot water and dip a rice paper round into it for a few seconds to soften. Place on a clean tea towel to drain.

- Place a heaped tablespoon of mixture towards the bottom of the wrap and spread it a little into a log shape.

- Fold the bottom edge over the mixture, bring in the sides and roll up tightly. Press to seal.

- Repeat with the remaining wrappers and mixture. Cover and chill for about 15 minutes. (The rolls can be made several hours ahead.)

- Serve with dipping sauce.

THAI SPRING ROLLS

These crispy spring rolls, jam packed with vegetables, are wonderful fresh and hot straight from the wok. A family favourite, I often make them with a range of different vegetables and a combination of prawns, minced pork and diced firm tofu.

Serves 4–6
Preparation and cooking time: 45 minutes

200 g (6 oz) uncooked prawns, finely chopped
200 g (6 oz) minced pork
1 cup bean sprouts
1 cup finely shredded cabbage
¼ cup Thai basil leaves, shredded
2 spring onions, sliced
1 tbsp fish sauce or soy sauce
1 tbsp red curry paste (page 44)
12 sheets frozen spring roll wrappers, thawed

Oil for deep frying

To serve: Thai sweet chilli sauce, either shop bought
or home-made (page 55)

- Place all the ingredients (except the wrappers) in a bowl and mix until well combined. Divide into 12 portions and shape each portion into a log about 10 cm (4 inches) long.

- Place a spring roll wrapper on the kitchen worktop with a corner facing you and place a 'log' of filling on that corner.

- Lift the corner of the wrapper over the log and roll up, folding the sides as you go. Brush the top corner with a little water and press down to seal. Repeat with the remaining filling and pastry.

- Deep fry the rolls in hot oil in two batches, for about 4 minutes per batch. Drain on kitchen paper and serve hot.

THAI STYLE CHICKEN WINGS

These are the perfect finger food with drinks or as part of a meal. They can be grilled or baked in the oven, and emerge with a sweet, spicy, garlicky glaze that tastes absolutely delicious. Try this recipe with chicken drumsticks for a more substantial dish.

Serves 4
Preparation and cooking time: 30 minutes
(plus marinating overnight)

20 chicken wings
2 tbsp soy sauce
2 tbsp oyster sauce
2 tbsp Thai sweet chilli sauce (page 55)
2 tbsp fish sauce
1 tbsp grated palm or soft brown sugar
1 tbsp minced garlic (bottled is fine)
1 tbsp lime juice
2 tsp chilli sauce or 1 fresh chilli, finely chopped
1 tbsp finely chopped coriander

- Cut the wings in half along the joint with a sharp knife and wash and drain well. Place them in a large bowl.

- Combine the remaining ingredients in a cup or small bowl and stir until the sugar dissolves.

- Pour the sauce over the chicken wings and mix well until all the chicken pieces are coated with the sauce. Cover and marinate overnight in the fridge. Remove the chicken from the fridge about 30 minutes before cooking.

- Pre-heat the oven to very hot – 230°C (210°C fan), 450°F or gas mark 8. Or pre-heat the grill.

- Place the wings on a rack in the oven or grill tray and cook them for about 15 minutes, turning once or twice and basting them with the leftover marinade.

- Serve hot.

THAI STYLE GARLIC PRAWNS

This tasty recipe is simple, quick and easy. It's the perfect way to serve fresh succulent prawns.

Note: Be careful when handling the chilli as it will irritate the skin and eyes. Wear thin rubber gloves and be careful not to touch your eyes. Or wash your hands thoroughly afterwards.

Serves 3–4
Preparation and cooking time: 25 minutes

500 g (1 lb) fresh king prawns, shelled tails left intact
1 large red chilli, seeded and finely chopped
2 cloves garlic, finely chopped
2 tsp fish sauce
1 tsp grated lime zest
2 tsp grated galangal or ginger
½ tsp ground cumin
1 tbsp oil
1 tbsp lime juice

- Combine all the ingredients except the lime juice in a bowl, cover and leave for about 5 minutes.

- Thread the prawns onto 4 metal (or pre-soaked wooden) skewers. Heat a cast iron pan or griddle until smoking and cook the prawns for 2–3 minutes, turning once.

- Sprinkle the lime juice over the prawns and serve at once.

COCONUT MILK BASED CURRIES

Coconut milk based curries are more common in the west than in Thai homes where they are likely to make an appearance only occasionally for more elaborate gatherings when a Pad Thai, a clear soup, a snack type dish and a spicy salad will also be included on the table, with diners helping themselves to a little of each dish.

THAI RED CURRY

This curry is richly aromatic and very, very tasty. Like all good Thai food, the fragrance and flavour of this curry are so delightful that it will lift your mood and give you a feeling of well being. You can make it with chicken, duck, pork, beef, tofu, prawns or a combination of these and a choice of fresh seasonal vegetables.

Serves 3–4
Preparation and cooking time: 45 minutes

200 ml (7 fl oz) coconut cream
3 tbsp red curry paste (page 44)
450 g (1 lb) chicken thigh fillets, trimmed and sliced
    into bite sized pieces
1 x 400 ml (14 fl oz) can of coconut milk
200 ml (7 fl oz) chicken stock (page 99, or hot water
    and ½ a stock cube)
2 tsp grated palm or soft brown sugar
1 red capsicum, de-seeded and sliced
2 carrots, peeled and thinly sliced
1 cup green beans, topped and tailed
4 kaffir lime leaves, shredded (or 1 tsp grated lime zest)
1 tbsp fish sauce
Small piece of galangal or ginger sliced into
    matchsticks (optional)
½ cup coriander leaves
½ cup Thai basil leaves

To serve: steamed jasmine rice, fish sauce, sliced
    chillies and lime wedges

- Heat the coconut cream in a wok or large pan on medium–high heat for 3–4 minutes until it starts to release the fat.

- Stir in the curry paste and cook for a minute or two until fragrant. Add the chicken and stir-fry until the chicken is opaque, about 3 minutes.

- Stir in the coconut milk, stock and sugar and bring to the boil. Turn down the heat, and simmer, stirring now and again, for 15 minutes. Add a little water at any time if the sauce is looking too dry.

- Add the vegetables and lime leaves (or zest) and return to the boil, cook on medium heat, uncovered, for about 5 minutes or until the vegetables are cooked and the chicken is tender.

- Stir in the fish sauce, turn off the heat and do the taste test. Add more fish sauce, sugar or chilli as desired.

- Stir through the galangal or ginger, half the coriander and basil. Ladle the curry into a large serving bowl and serve sprinkled with the remaining coriander and basil.

THAI SEAFOOD CURRY

This curry is a healthy and tasty one-pot wonder that will delight lovers of seafood. It is really quick to cook too.

Serves 4
Preparation and cooking time: 25 minutes

1 tbsp oil
3 tbsp red curry paste (page 44)
1 tsp ground coriander
1 tsp ground cumin
1 x 400 ml (14 fl oz) can coconut milk
2 tsp tamarind paste
1 tsp grated palm or soft brown sugar
1 red or green capsicum, cut into chunks
1 courgette (zucchini) cut into chunks
6 cherry tomatoes
450 g (1 lb) mixed seafood (chunks of salmon, prawns, scallops, mussels)
2 tsp fish sauce
½ cup coriander leaves
1 cup lemon basil leaves

To serve: steamed jasmine rice or stir-fried rice with pineapple (page 158). Fish sauce, sliced chillies, lemon or lime wedges

- Heat the oil in a wok or large pan on medium-high heat and add the curry paste and ground spices. Stir-fry for about a minute.

- Stir in the coconut milk, tamarind paste and sugar and bring to the boil. Turn down the heat, and simmer, stirring now and again, for about 5 minutes.

- Add the vegetables and 1 cup of water and return to the boil, cook on medium heat, uncovered, for a further 5 minutes.

- Stir in the seafood and simmer gently for 5–6 minutes until the seafood is cooked through.

- Add the fish sauce, turn off the heat and do the taste test. Add more sugar, fish sauce, lime or lemon juice if required.

- Stir through half the coriander and basil. Ladle the curry into a large serving bowl and serve sprinkled with the remaining coriander and basil.

RED CURRY WITH BAMBOO SHOOTS

This is an easy and delicious curry that goes well with plain, steamed jasmine rice. Try it with beef or pork instead of chicken and use any vegetables you like.

Note: Be careful when handling chillies as they will irritate the skin and eyes. Wear thin rubber gloves and be careful not to touch your eyes. Or wash your hands thoroughly afterwards.

Serves 4
Preparation and cooking time: 35 minutes

1 x 400 ml (14 fl oz) can coconut milk
3 tbsp red curry paste (page 44)
450 g (1 lb) chicken thigh fillets, trimmed and sliced
    into bite sized pieces
2 tsp grated palm or soft brown sugar
1 cup sliced green beans
1 cup sliced bamboo shoots
4 kaffir lime leaves, halved (or 1 tsp grated lime zest)
2 tsp fish sauce
2 large red chillies, seeded and sliced lengthways into
    long strips
1 cup Thai basil leaves

To serve: steamed jasmine rice, fish sauce, sliced chillies,
    lime wedges

- Heat half the coconut milk in a wok or large pan on medium-high heat and add the curry paste and stir until combined.

- Add the chicken, bring to the boil and simmer for about 5 minutes.

- Stir in the remaining coconut milk, half a cup of water and the sugar and bring to the boil.

- Turn down the heat, and simmer, stirring now and again, for a further 10 minutes.

- Add the beans, bamboo shoots, lime leaves (or zest) and return to the boil, cook on medium heat, uncovered, for about 5 minutes or until the chicken and beans are tender.

- Stir in the fish sauce, turn off the heat and do the taste test. Add more fish sauce, sugar or chilli as desired.

- Stir through half the sliced chillies and basil. Ladle the curry into a large bowl and serve sprinkled with the remaining chilli and basil.

RED DUCK CURRY WITH LYCHEES

The hot and spicy paste, the lusciously sweet lychees, the salty fish sauce and the creamy richness of the coconut all combine to make this a deliciously memorable dish.

Serves 4
Preparation and cooking time: 35 minutes

½ Chinese roast duck*
1 x 400 ml (14 fl oz) can coconut cream
4 tbsp red curry paste (page 44)
1 x 400 ml (14 fl oz) can coconut milk
1 cup canned lychees in syrup, drained
4 kaffir lime leaves, halved (or 1 tsp grated lime zest)
3 tsp fish sauce
1 cup Thai basil leaves
½ cup coriander leaves

To serve: steamed jasmine rice, a vegetable side dish,
    fish sauce, lime wedges and sliced red chilli

- Remove the skin from the duck, remove the flesh from the bones and slice into bite sized pieces.

- Place the coconut cream in a wok or large pan and bring to the boil. Cook stirring over medium heat until the oil starts to separate from it, about 5 minutes.

- Add the curry paste, stir until combined and cook for about 2 minutes.

- Stir in the coconut milk, a little at a time, bringing it to the boil each time.

- Add all the remaining ingredients except for the basil and coriander and bring slowly to the boil again.

- Turn off the heat and do the taste test. Add more fish sauce, sugar or chilli as desired.

- Stir through the basil, sprinkle with the coriander and serve.

*Tip: *If you can't get roast duck and still want to make this dish, you can buy duck breasts from the supermarket and roast them yourself: score the skin with a sharp knife, season well, place in a baking dish and roast in a hot oven (220°C/200°C fan/425°F/gas mark 7) for about 15 minutes. Allow to rest for at least 15 minutes before removing the skin and slicing the meat.*

RED BEEF CURRY WITH AUBERGINE

Aubergines (eggplants) are widely used in Thai cuisine and come in all shapes, colours and sizes ranging from the tiny dark green pea one to the larger green, yellow, purple, white and even striped fruits. The flavour of Thai aubergine is quite different from the varieties available in the west as is the texture. However, western and Japanese varieties can be successfully substituted unless you are fortunate enough to be able to buy Thai aubergines.

This is a delicious curry that requires less meat than usual because of the generous helping of aubergine. The addition of green peppercorns gives it texture and a lovely peppery flavour.

Note: Be careful when handling the chilli as it will irritate the skin and eyes. Wear thin rubber gloves and be careful not to touch your eyes. Or wash your hands thoroughly afterwards.

Serves 4–6
Preparation and cooking time: 40 minutes

3 tbsp oil
300 g (10 oz) aubergine, cut into chunks
200 ml (7 fl oz) coconut cream
4 tbsp red curry paste
300 g (10 oz) lean beef, thinly sliced
250 ml (8 fl oz) coconut milk
3–4 small stems green peppercorns or 1 tbsp green peppercorns
    in brine, rinsed
6 kaffir lime leaves, halved (or 1½ tsp grated lime zest)
1 large red chilli, sliced diagonally
2 tbsp fish sauce
1 tbsp soy sauce
2 tsp grated palm or soft brown sugar
1 cup Thai basil leaves

To serve: rice or noodles, fish sauce, sliced chilli
    and lime wedges

- Combine the oil and aubergine in a large bowl and stir until all the pieces are coated with oil.

- Heat a wok or large pan on high heat until almost smoking and add half the aubergine and stir-fry for about 3 minutes. Transfer to a plate and repeat with the remaining aubergine.

- Wipe the wok clean with kitchen towel and add the coconut cream, reserving about 2 tablespoons. Bring the coconut cream to the boil and cook on medium heat for about 4 minutes or until it starts to release the oil.

- Stir in the curry paste and cook for about a minute. Add the beef and stir-fry about 2 minutes.

- Add the aubergine chunks to the beef, together with all the remaining ingredients except for the basil leaves and the reserved coconut cream. Stir well, bring to the boil and simmer for about 2 minutes.

- Stir in half the basil leaves. Turn off the heat and do the taste test. Add more sugar, chilli or fish sauce as required.

- Serve sprinkled with the remaining basil and drizzled with the reserved coconut cream.

CLASSIC THAI GREEN CURRY

This delicious, creamy and aromatic green curry recipe is cooked with chicken but it can also be prepared with pork, beef or fish.

Note: Be careful when handling chillies as they will irritate the skin and eyes. Wear thin rubber gloves and be careful not to touch your eyes. Or wash your hands thoroughly afterwards.

Serves 4
Preparation and cooking time: 35 minutes

1 tbsp oil
3 tbsp green curry paste (page 46)
1 x 400 ml (14 fl oz) can of coconut milk
450 g (1 lb) chicken thigh fillets, trimmed and sliced
3 kaffir lime leaves (or 1 tsp grated lime zest)
200 ml (7 fl oz) coconut cream
1 tbsp fish sauce
2 tsp grated palm or soft brown sugar
3 small courgettes (zucchini) sliced
2–3 hot red chillies, seeded and sliced into long strips
¼ cup sweet basil leaves

To serve: steamed jasmine rice or vegetable fried rice,
   fish sauce, sliced chilli and lime wedges

- Heat the oil in a wok or large pan over medium heat and add the curry paste. Cook for 2–3 minutes until fragrant.

- Reduce the heat a little and add the coconut milk a little at a time, bringing it to a simmer before adding more. Stir and cook until an oily film forms over the top.

- Stir in the chicken and lime leaves (or zest) and stir-fry for about 5 minutes or until the chicken is cooked through.

- Add the coconut cream, fish sauce and sugar and bring to the boil. Add the sliced courgettes and cook for a further 5 minutes.

- Turn off the heat and do the taste test. Add more fish sauce, sugar or chilli as desired.

- Ladle the curry into a serving dish and sprinkle over the sliced chilli and basil leaves. Serve.

THAI YELLOW CURRY

This curry is made with the addition of Thai curry powder and is not dissimilar to Indian curries. The chicken and potatoes in the mildly spiced, creamy sauce make this a delicious and satisfying dish.

Serves 4
Preparation and cooking time: 35 minutes

2 medium potatoes, peeled
250 ml (1 cup/8 fl oz) coconut cream
4 tbsp yellow curry paste (page 48)
1 tsp Thai curry powder*
350 g (12 oz) chicken breast, thinly sliced
250 ml (1 cup/8 fl oz) coconut milk
1 tbsp grated palm or soft brown sugar
1 tbsp light soy sauce
¼ cup coriander leaves (optional)

To serve: steamed jasmine rice, green mango salad (page 180), fish or soy sauce, sliced chilli

- Cut the potatoes into smallish chunks and boil in salted water for about 5 minutes or until just cooked. Drain.

- Meanwhile, place the coconut cream in a wok over medium heat and cook for 3 or 4 minutes until the oil floats to the surface.

- Stir in the curry paste and curry powder and cook for a further 2 minutes.

- Add the chicken and potato and stir-fry for about 3 minutes or until the chicken turns opaque.

- Add the coconut milk and sugar, bring back to the boil and simmer for a further 5 minutes or until the potato is really tender and the chicken is cooked through.

- Stir in the soy sauce. Turn off the heat and do the taste test. Add more soy sauce, sugar or chilli as desired.

- Serve sprinkled with the coriander leaves if using.

*Thai curry powder: *4 cinnamon sticks, 4 tsp yellow mustard seeds, 4 tsp white pepper, 2 tbsp turmeric. Grind the cinnamon and seeds to a fine powder in an electric coffee grinder or pestle and mortar and combine with the turmeric. Store in an airtight container in a cool place for up to 2 months.*

PANANG BEEF CURRY

Flavour packed Panang curry doesn't have as much sauce as the typical Thai curry and doesn't usually contain any vegetables. Beef is the meat of choice but chicken and pork make a delicious change.

Note: Be careful when handling the chilli as it will irritate the skin and eyes. Wear thin rubber gloves and be careful not to touch your eyes. Or wash your hands thoroughly afterwards.

Serves 4
Preparation and cooking time: 35 minutes

1 x 400 ml (14 fl oz) can of coconut milk
200 ml (6 fl oz) coconut cream
3 tbsp Panang curry paste (page 50)
450 g (1 lb) rump steak, sliced into bite sized pieces
3 kaffir lime leaves, shredded (or 1 tsp grated lime zest)
1 tbsp grated palm or brown sugar
¼ cup ground roasted peanuts
2 tbsp fish sauce
1 large red chilli, sliced

To serve: rice, a vegetable side dish, fish or soy sauce, sliced chillies

- Place half the coconut milk and all the cream in a wok or large pan and simmer for about 5 minutes or until a film of oil forms on the surface.

- Turn up the heat a little and add the curry paste. Cook, stirring, for 2 minutes until fragrant and add the beef and lime leaves or zest.

- Bring to the boil and simmer, stirring now and again, for about 5 minutes before adding in the remainder of the coconut milk, sugar and peanuts.

- Bring to the boil again, and simmer, stirring now and again, for about 15 minutes or until the beef is tender. Add a little water if the pan is drying out too much. Stir in the fish sauce.

- Turn off the heat and do the taste test. Add more fish sauce, sugar or chilli as desired.

- Transfer to a serving dish and garnish with the sliced chilli.

Tip: *The ground peanuts help thicken the curry as well as add flavour. Use ground almonds or cashews if you are allergic to peanuts, or omit altogether.*

MASSAMAN CURRY

Massaman or Thai Muslim curry is milder and more aromatic than most other Thai curries. The warm and pungent spices of the Indian subcontinent combined with fragrant lemongrass, galangal and kaffir lime make it a rich and hearty dish. Generally made with beef, Massaman curry is just as good with pork, chicken or lamb. This curry is best eaten the next day to allow the flavours to develop.

Serves 4
Preparation and cooking time: 50–60 minutes

1 x 400 ml (14 fl oz) can coconut milk
450 g (1 lb) rump steak, sliced into 2.5 cm (1 inch) chunks
1 fresh or dried bay leaf
6 cardamom pods
3 cloves
1 x 2.5 cm (1 inch) stick cinnamon
4 medium potatoes, peeled and cut into 2.5 cm (1 inch) chunks
250 ml (1 cup/8 fl oz) coconut cream
3 tbsp Massaman curry paste (page 43)
2 tbsp roasted peanuts, roughly chopped (optional)
2 tbsp grated palm or soft brown sugar
2 tbsp fish sauce
2 tbsp tamarind paste
2 tbsp lime juice

To serve: rice, a vegetable side dish, fish sauce, sliced chillies

- Heat the coconut milk in a heavy based saucepan until boiling and add the sliced beef, bay leaf, cardamom pods, cloves and cinnamon stick. Add a cup of hot water, reduce the heat and simmer for 30–35 minutes or until the meat is tender.

- Meanwhile, cook the potatoes in boiling salted water until just tender. Drain and set aside.

- Heat the coconut cream in a wok or large pan and cook, stirring, until the oil separates.

- Add the curry paste and cook for 2 minutes until fragrant. Transfer to the pan with the beef and add the peanuts, sugar and potatoes.

- Bring back to the boil and simmer for 10 minutes before stirring in the remaining ingredients. Simmer for a further 2 minutes.

- Turn off the heat and do the taste test. Add more fish sauce, sugar, lime juice or chilli as desired.

- Transfer to a serving dish and serve hot.

WATER BASED CURRIES

Water based curries are eaten with regularity throughout Thailand, always with plenty of steamed jasmine rice. They are traditionally hotter than the coconut based curries and commonly have a sourer element. A good water based curry has plenty of flavour from the inclusion of lots of very flavoursome ingredients and fresh herbs.

TRADITIONAL THAI PORK CURRY

This is a delicious pork curry popular in northern Thailand. If there's enough time, cook it the day before to allow the lovely flavours to develop and serve with steamed greens and jasmine rice for a tasty and authentic meal.

Serves 4
Preparation and cooking time: 2 hours (plus marinating time)

500g trimmed pork shoulder, cut into 2.5 cm
   (1 inch) chunks
4 tbsp red curry paste (page 44)
2 tbsp fish sauce
2 tbsp soy sauce
2 tbsp grated palm or soft brown sugar
2 tbsp roasted peanuts, roughly chopped
1 tbsp tamarind paste
2 tsp Thai curry powder (page 83)
3 tbsp oil
Small piece galangal or ginger, sliced into matchsticks
½ cup Thai basil leaves

To serve: rice, fish sauce, chilli sauce and lime wedges

- Combine the pork, curry paste, sauces, sugar, peanuts, tamarind and curry powder in a large bowl and leave to marinate for about 2 hours or overnight.

- Heat the oil in a wok or large pan and fry the pork for 3 or 4 minutes until it colours. Add a litre (2.2 pints) of hot water and bring to boil.

- Simmer, partly covered, for about 1–1½ hours until the pork is tender. Add more water as required.

- Before serving, do the taste test and add more fish or soy sauce or sugar as desired.

- Serve sprinkled with the ginger and basil leaves.

JUNGLE CURRY

This delicious curry originates from the country regions of Thailand where it is still prepared with wild boar. Chicken or pork are good alternatives as is tofu if you want to prepare a vegetarian version.

Serves 4
Preparation and cooking time: 30 minutes

2 tbsp oil
3 tbsp green curry paste (page 46)
1 bay leaf, torn into 2 or 3 pieces
450 g (1 lb) chicken or pork fillet, sliced into bite sized pieces
2 tbsp sliced bamboo shoots (canned)
2 small, long aubergines (eggplants), sliced
400 ml (10 fl oz) hot chicken stock (page 99)
1 tbsp fish sauce
1 tbsp lime juice
1 tbsp chopped coriander
3 small stems green peppercorn (or 1 tbsp canned green
    peppercorns in brine, drained)
Small piece of galangal or ginger, sliced into matchsticks
½ cup holy basil leaves

To serve: steamed jasmine rice, fish sauce, chilli sauce
    and lime wedges

- Heat the oil in a wok or deep frying pan over medium–high heat and add the curry paste and bay leaf.

- Stir-fry for a minute or two until aromatic and add the meat. Stir-fry for 3 minutes.

- Add the bamboo shoots and aubergine and stir-fry for about a minute or until well coated with the paste.

- Add the stock and bring to the boil. Simmer gently for about 10 minutes.

- Stir in the fish sauce and lime juice and do the taste test. Add more lime juice or fish sauce as desired.

- Stir through the coriander, peppercorns and galangal or ginger. Serve in a deep bowl, garnished with the basil leaves.

SLOW COOKED BEEF CURRY

This curry is prepared with tougher but more flavoursome cuts of beef that allow for long slow cooking. It has delicious, complex flavours that get even better if the dish is left for a day before being eaten.

Serves 4
Preparation and cooking time: 3 hours

2 tbsp oil
4 tbsp red curry paste (page 44)
450 g (1 lb) stewing beef, cut into 2.5 cm (1 inch) chunks
500 ml (1 pt) beef stock or consommé
1 bay leaf
1 x 2.5 cm (1 inch) stick cinnamon
2 tbsp grated palm or soft brown sugar
2 tbsp soy sauce
2 tbsp fish sauce
Juice of 1 lime
1 cup shredded iceberg lettuce
2 cups bean sprouts
1 spring onion, sliced
1 cup coriander leaves

To serve: steamed jasmine rice or noodles and hot and sour sauce – stir 2 tbsp caster sugar into ½ cup of rice vinegar until dissolved. Add 2 or more finely sliced chillies of choice.

- Heat the oil in a large, heavy based pan over medium heat and add the curry paste. Cook for a minute or two until fragrant and stir in the beef.

- Stir-fry the beef for two minutes and add the stock, 500 ml (1 pt) water, bay leaf, cinnamon and sugar.

- Bring to the boil and simmer, covered for 2–2½ hours or until the meat is very tender.

- Stir in the sauces and lime juice, turn off the heat and do the taste test. Add more fish sauce, sugar, lime juice or chilli as desired.

- Divide the lettuce and bean sprouts into 4 individual serving bowls and ladle on the beef curry.

- Sprinkle with spring onion and coriander and serve with rice or noodles and hot and sour sauce.

SWEET AND SOUR CHICKEN CURRY

The tasty richness of the stock in this curry is due to the chicken bones being left in the meat. You can use thigh fillets and chicken stock if you prefer, but to get the best of this dish, you will need to use a whole chicken or chicken hindquarters, bones and all. Get your butcher to chop the chicken or hindquarters into small pieces. You can leave the skin on too if you wish, although I prefer to remove it.

Note: Be careful when handling chillies as they will irritate the skin and eyes. Wear thin rubber gloves and be careful not to touch your eyes. Or wash your hands thoroughly afterwards.

Serves 4
Preparation and cooking time: 40 minutes

2 tbsp oil
750 g (1½ lb) chicken pieces with bone in
3 tbsp red curry paste (page 44)
2 tbsp tamarind paste
Juice of one lime
3 kaffir lime leaves or 1 tsp grated lime zest
3 tbsp grated palm or soft brown sugar
2 cups shredded Chinese cabbage
1 tbsp soy sauce
2 tbsp fish sauce
2–3 long red chillies, sliced on the diagonal
½ cup Thai basil leaves

To serve: rice, fish sauce, chilli sauce and lime wedges

- Heat the oil in a wok or large pan and fry the chicken pieces in two batches for about 5 minutes or until browned.

- Add the curry paste and stir-fry for 2 minutes or until the paste is fragrant.

- Stir in the tamarind, lime juice, lime leaves or zest and sugar with enough water to cover and stir over medium heat until the sugar dissolves.

- Bring to the boil and simmer gently for about 20 minutes or until the chicken is tender.

- Add the cabbage, soy sauce and fish sauce and simmer for a further 5 minutes.

- Turn off the heat and do the taste test. Add more fish sauce, sugar or chilli as desired.

- Ladle into a serving bowl and scatter the sliced chillies and basil leaves over the top. Serve with steamed jasmine rice.

SOUR YELLOW CURRY WITH SALMON

Sour fish curry is a delicacy of southern Thailand traditionally cooked with fresh, locally caught fish. This recipe uses salmon for a slightly westernized version of the delicious dish but you can use any fresh fish.

Substitute the asparagus with sliced green beans if preferred.

Note: Be careful when handling chillies as they will irritate the skin and eyes. Wear thin rubber gloves and be careful not to touch your eyes. Or wash your hands thoroughly afterwards.

Serves 4
Preparation and cooking time: 20 minutes
(plus marinating time)

4 tbsp yellow curry paste (page 48)
1 tsp turmeric
4 salmon fillets or cutlets
2 tbsp oil
1 bunch asparagus, sliced into 2.5 cm (1 inch) lengths
2 tbsp tamarind paste, dissolved in 2 cups warm water
2 tbsp lemon juice
2 tsp grated palm or soft brown sugar
1 cup pineapple chunks
4 kaffir lime leaves, shredded (or 1 tsp grated lime zest)
2 long red chillies, sliced

To serve: rice, fish sauce, chilli sauce and lime or lemon wedges

- Combine the curry paste and turmeric in a large dish and smother the salmon pieces with the mixture. Set aside for about 15 minutes if time allows.

- Heat the oil in a frying pan large enough to take the salmon pieces in a single layer. Add the salmon and cook over medium heat for about 1 minute each side.

- Add the asparagus, tamarind water, lemon juice, sugar and pineapple and bring to a simmer.

- Cook for about 6–8 minutes, depending on the thickness of the fish, turning once.

- Serve sprinkled with the lime leaves or zest and chillies.

SPICY BASIL CHICKEN

This is a quick and easy curry with the lovely aroma of basil and a powerful chilli hit. Not for the faint hearted. It's particularly good when made with real, home-made chicken stock.

Note: Be careful when handling chillies as they will irritate the skin and eyes. Wear thin rubber gloves and be careful not to touch your eyes. Or wash your hands thoroughly afterwards.

Serves 4
Preparation and cooking time: 25 minutes

1 tbsp oil
450 g (1 lb) chicken thigh fillets, trimmed and thinly sliced
3 tbsp green curry paste (page 46)
1 green capsicum, de-seeded and sliced
2 Thai or other hot green chillies, finely sliced
1½ cups Thai basil leaves
2 cups chicken stock (page 99)
1 tbsp grated palm or soft brown sugar
1 tbsp hot chilli sauce or 1 tsp chilli powder
2 tbsp fish sauce
2 tbsp lime juice

To serve: rice, fish sauce, chilli sauce and lime wedges

- Heat the oil in a wok or large pan and stir-fry the chicken for about 2 minutes or until opaque.

- Add the curry paste and capsicum and stir-fry for about a minute or until fragrant.

- Stir in the chillies and about two-thirds of the basil, stir-fry for about 30 seconds and add the stock and sugar.

- Bring to the boil and simmer gently for about 10 minutes. Stir in the chilli sauce or powder, fish sauce and lime juice.

- Turn off the heat and do the taste test. Add more fish sauce, lime juice or chilli as desired.

- Serve sprinkled with the remaining basil.

Real Chicken Stock – *makes about 2 litres (3½ pints) and freezes well for up to 3 months. You will need a large stock pot or saucepan for this, but it is easy to make and you can really taste the difference.*

About 3 kg (6½ lb chicken bones)
5 litres (11 pints) water
1 onion, roughly chopped
1 stick celery, roughly chopped
1 carrot, roughly chopped
1 tsp black peppercorns

Rinse the bones in cold water, place in the stock pot with all the remaining ingredients. Bring to the boil and simmer very gently for about 3 hours. Skim the top now and again. Cool the stock and strain through muslin or a fine strainer, into a clean container. Place in the fridge overnight. In the morning, remove and discard the fat that will have set at the top. The stock is now ready to use or freeze.

SOUR PRAWN CURRY

Another popular dish in Thailand, this traditional curry is great when you have access to really good, fresh prawns. If not, try it with chunks of fresh, white fish.

Note: Be careful when handling chillies as they will irritate the skin and eyes. Wear thin rubber gloves and be careful not to touch your eyes. Or wash your hands thoroughly afterwards.

Serves 4
Preparation and cooking time: 30 minutes
(plus marinating time)

20–24 king prawns, peeled with tails intact
1 tbsp sesame oil
1 tbsp grated galangal or ginger
4 tbsp red curry paste (page 44)
1 litre (4 cups/2.2 pints) chicken stock (page 99)
1 cup chopped green vegetables (e.g. beans, snow
    peas/mangetout, broccoli, pak choi/bok choy)
2 tbsp tamarind paste
2 tbsp fish sauce
Juice of 1 lemon
1 tbsp grated palm or soft brown sugar
1 cup pineapple chunks
2 long red chillies, sliced
½ cup coriander leaves (optional)

To serve: rice or noodles, fish sauce, sliced chillies, lime
    or lemon wedges

- Combine the prawns with the oil, galangal or ginger and curry paste and leave to marinate for about 15 minutes if time allows.

- Heat a wok or large pan and stir-fry the prawn mixture for about 2 minutes or until the prawns colour. Remove from the wok/pan and set aside.

- Add the stock to the wok/pan and bring to the boil. Add the vegetables and simmer for a minute.

- Stir in the prawns, tamarind, fish sauce, lemon juice, sugar and pineapple and simmer for a further 2 minutes or until the prawns are cooked through and the vegetables are tender crisp.

- Stir through the chillies, turn off the heat and do the taste test. Add more fish sauce, sugar, lemon juice or chilli as desired.

- Serve sprinkled with the coriander if using.

HOT AND SOUR SEAFOOD CURRY

In Thailand this unusual curry is often eaten with strips of a specially made vegetable omelette stirred through it. In this recipe, I've stirred the egg through the stock at the last minute. This helps thicken the sauce and provides tasty shreds of egg.

Serves 4
Preparation and cooking time: 35 minutes

450 g (1 lb) mixed seafood (prawns, mussels, octopus, etc)
3 tbsp red curry paste (page 44)
2 tbsp oil
200 g (7 oz) white fish fillet
3 tbsp tamarind paste
1 litre (2 cups/2.2 pints) chicken or fish stock
2 cups shredded Chinese cabbage
Juice of 1 lemon
2 tsp grated palm or soft brown sugar
½–1 tsp chilli powder
2 eggs, beaten
3 tbsp fish sauce
½ cup coriander leaves

To serve: rice, fish sauce, chilli sauce and lime wedges

- Combine the seafood with the curry paste and oil and mix well. Set aside.

- Simmer the fish in lightly salted water until it begins to flake. Drain, cool slightly and remove any skin and bones.

- Mash the fish with a fork, combine with the tamarind paste and process until smooth using a food processor or a pestle and mortar.

- Heat a wok or large pan and stir-fry the seafood for about a minute. Add the stock and bring to the boil.

- Add the cabbage and simmer for 3–4 minutes or until the seafood is cooked.

- Stir through the fish and tamarind paste, lemon juice, sugar and chilli powder. Simmer for a further minute.

- Slide the beaten egg into the curry whilst stirring rapidly to produce shreds of cooked egg. Stir in the fish sauce.

- Turn off the heat and do the taste test. Add more fish sauce, sugar, lemon juice or chilli as desired.

- Stir through half the coriander and serve with the remaining coriander sprinkled over the top.

THAI BRAISED BEEF CURRY

This is a deliciously hearty dish that can be eaten as a satisfying soup with crusty bread or as part of a Thai meal with noodles or rice.

Serves 4–6
Preparation and cooking time: 2–2½ hours

2 tbsp oil
3 tbsp red curry paste (page 44)
450 g (1 lb) braising beef, sliced into 2.5 cm (1 inch) chunks
1 onion, sliced
1 stick celery, sliced into 2.5 cm (1 inch) lengths
2 cups beef stock
1 x 2.5 cm (1 inch) stick cinnamon
1 bay leaf
2 cups shredded Chinese cabbage
1 tsp freshly ground black pepper
3 tbsp fish sauce
2 cups bean sprouts
½ cup coriander leaves
1 tbsp fried garlic (optional)

To serve: rice, fish sauce, chilli sauce or sliced chillies and
    lime wedges

- Heat the oil in a large heavy based pan over medium heat and stir-fry the curry paste for a minute or until fragrant.

- Turn up the heat and add the beef, onion and celery. Stir-fry for 3 minutes.

- Stir through the stock and 1½ litres (6 cups/3.3 pints) hot water.

- Bring to the boil and add the cinnamon and bay leaf. Simmer for 1½–2 hours or until the meat is very tender.

- Stir through the cabbage, black pepper and fish sauce. Simmer for a further 10 minutes or until the cabbage is tender.

- Turn off the heat and do the taste test. Add more fish sauce or chilli as desired.

- Divide the bean sprouts amongst 4 serving bowls and ladle the beef curry over the top.

- Garnish with the coriander leaves and fried garlic if using.

EASY STIR-FRIES

From combinations of fresh, local vegetables, to those that include meat, fish or tofu, stir-fries are commonplace in daily Thai cooking. Although Thai stir-fries have some similarities with Chinese stir-fries, the flavours and aromas of the Thai variety are much more intense due to the liberal use of lime, galangal, lemongrass and other delicious herbs and spices.

Remember, everything happens quickly with stir-fires so preparation is the key.

BASIL CHICKEN STIR-FRY

This dish is a favourite in Thai homes where it is often served for breakfast or lunch topped with a fried egg. It is very quick and easy to prepare and is great with pork or prawns as well as chicken.

Slicing the meat thinly helps it cook quickly and absorb the delicious flavours.

Note: Be careful when handling chillies as they will irritate the skin and eyes. Wear thin rubber gloves and be careful not to touch your eyes. Or wash your hands thoroughly afterwards.

Serves 3–4
Preparation and cooking time: 20 minutes

Stir-Fry Sauce: In a small bowl or cup combine 2 tsp dark soy sauce, 1 tsp grated palm or soft brown sugar and 2 tbsp fish sauce. Stir until the sugar dissolves and set aside.

2 tbsp oil
4 cloves garlic, finely chopped
2 shallots or ½ onion, finely chopped
450 g (1 lb) chicken thigh fillets, sliced into small bite
   sized pieces
2 kaffir lime leaves, thinly sliced or 1 tsp finely grated lime zest
2–4 Thai (or other hot) red chillies, finely sliced
1 cup holy basil or sweet basil leaves
1 red chilli extra, sliced on the diagonal
½ cup mint leaves

To serve: steamed jasmine rice, fish sauce, hot sauce,
   lime wedges
1 tbsp fried garlic (optional)

- Heat a wok or large deep frying pan on high until smoking and add the oil. Swirl the oil around to coat the wok or pan and heat for a few more seconds.

- Add the garlic, stir once and add the shallots or onion. Stir-fry for 10–15 seconds.

- Add the chicken and stir-fry for about 3–4 minutes or until the chicken pieces are coloured and cooked through.

- Stir in the lime leaves or zest and chillies and stir-fry for about 20 seconds.

- Add the prepared sauce and stir-fry until combined.

- Stir through the basil leaves and turn off the heat.

- Transfer to a serving dish and sprinkle over the extra chilli and mint leaves.

CASHEW CHICKEN STIR-FRY

This delicious and healthy recipe originated with the Chinese but, with the inclusion of lemongrass, fish sauce and other Thai style ingredients, it has developed the lovely flavours typical of Thai cuisine.

Note: Be careful when handling chillies as they will irritate the skin and eyes. Wear thin rubber gloves and be careful not to touch your eyes. Or wash your hands thoroughly afterwards.

Serves 4
Preparation and cooking time: 35 minutes

Stir-Fry Sauce: In a bowl or jug combine 1 cup chicken stock, 2 tbsp lime juice, 2 tbsp light soy sauce, 2 tbsp fish sauce, 2 tbsp finely sliced lemongrass (fresh or frozen), 1 tbsp grated palm or soft brown sugar and 2 tsp cornflour mixed with 2 tbsp water. Stir until the sugar dissolves and set aside.

2 tbsp oil
3 cloves garlic, finely sliced
1 onion, sliced
2–3 Thai (or other hot) red chillies, finely sliced (optional)
450 g (1 lb) chicken thigh or breast fillets, trimmed and sliced into strips
½ cup sliced mushrooms
1 cup sliced pak choi/bok choy or other greens
3 spring onions, sliced into 2.5 cm (1 inch) lengths
½ cup roasted cashews

To serve: rice, fish sauce, chilli sauce or sliced chillies and lime wedges

- Heat a wok or large deep frying pan on high until smoking and add the oil. Swirl the oil around to coat the wok or pan and heat for a few more seconds.

- Add the garlic, stir once and add the onion and chillies if using. Stir-fry for 10–15 seconds.

- Add the chicken and mushrooms, and stir-fry for 4–5 minutes until well coloured and cooked through.

- Add a splash of water and stir in the pak choi and spring onions and stir-fry for a further minute until they turn bright green.

- Add the cashews and the stir-fry sauce and bring to the boil, stirring until the sauce thickens. Cook for a few more seconds and take off the heat.

- Do the taste test. The sauce should be tangy with a little sweetness. Add fish sauce, sugar or lime juice if required.

- Serve with rice or noodles.

CHICKEN AND GINGER STIR-FRY

This is a simple but delicious dish with the lively flavour and fragrance of fresh ginger. The addition of lots of crisp, fresh vegetables makes it healthy too.

Note: Be careful when handling chillies as they will irritate the skin and eyes. Wear thin rubber gloves and be careful not to touch your eyes. Or wash your hands thoroughly afterwards.

Serves 4
Preparation and cooking time: 35 minutes

Stir-Fry Sauce: In a small bowl or cup combine 2 tbsp soy sauce, 2 tbsp fish sauce, 1 tbsp rice vinegar, 1 tsp grated palm or soft brown sugar and 1 tsp cornflour mixed with 2 tbsp water. Stir until the sugar dissolves and set aside.

2 tbsp oil
3 cloves garlic, finely sliced
1 small onion, sliced
2–3 red chillies, finely sliced
1/3 cup julienned ginger
450 g (1 lb) chicken thigh fillets, trimmed and thinly sliced
½ cup sliced mushrooms
1 cup mixed greens (pak choi/bok choy or Asian greens)
1 cup snow peas (mangetout), trimmed
½ cup basil leaves

To serve: rice, fish sauce, chilli sauce or sliced chillies and lime wedges

- Heat a wok or large deep frying pan on high until smoking and add the oil. Swirl the oil around to coat the wok or pan and heat for a few more seconds.

- Add the garlic, stir once and add the onion, chillies and half the ginger. Stir-fry for 10–15 seconds.

- Add the chicken and mushrooms and stir-fry for 6–8 minutes until the chicken is coloured and cooked through.

- Add the remaining ginger and vegetables to the wok with about half a cup of water and stir-fry for 2 minutes until the vegetables soften a little.

- Stir through the stir-fry sauce and cook, stirring, until thickened.

- Turn off the heat and do the taste test. Add fish sauce, sugar or chilli as desired.

- Transfer to a serving dish and sprinkle the basil leaves over.

CRISPY HERB AND BEEF STIR-FRY

This is a stir-fry with robust garlic and herb flavours that combine beautifully with beef. It is a spectacular dish for lovers of really flavoursome food.

Don't worry about the quantity of oil as most of it is drained off. Don't discard it though as it will be full of flavour and great for future curries or stir-fries.

Note: Be careful when handling chillies as they will irritate the skin and eyes. Wear thin rubber gloves and be careful not to touch your eyes. Or wash your hands thoroughly afterwards.

Serves 4
Preparation and cooking time: 45 minutes

450 g (1 lb) rump or sirloin steak, sliced into thin strips
3 kaffir lime leaves (or 1 tsp grated lime zest)
1 tbsp roast chilli paste (page 52)
1 cup oil
6 shallots or 2 onions, finely sliced
8 cloves garlic, finely sliced
½ cup cashew nuts, unroasted
3 tbsp grated galangal or ginger
3 tbsp finely sliced lemongrass, white part only
1 cup holy basil leaves
2 tsp grated palm or soft brown sugar dissolved in 2 tbsp warm water
3–4 red chillies, sliced
2 tbsp fish sauce

To serve: rice, fish sauce, chilli sauce or sliced chillies and lime wedges

- Combine the beef, lime leaves or zest and chilli paste in a bowl. Cover and set aside.

- Heat the oil in a wok or large pan over high heat and fry the shallots or onions for about 2 minutes until starting to turn golden at the edges.

- Add the garlic, cashew nuts, galangal and lemongrass and fry for a further 2 minutes until crisp, adding the basil leaves for the final 30 seconds.

- Drain with a slotted spoon and set aside. Carefully remove all but about 2 tbsp of the oil and reserve for another use.

- Heat the wok/pan again until smoking and add the beef. Stir-fry for 3–4 minutes until browned and just cooked through.

- Stir through the sugar, chillies and fish sauce and mix over medium heat until well combined. Turn heat to low and toss through the fried herbs.

- Turn off the heat and do the taste test. Add more fish sauce, sugar or chilli as desired.

PORK, LONG BEANS AND CURRY PASTE STIR-FRY

Long beans, or yard long beans, are common in Thai and Chinese cooking. Also known as snake beans, garter beans and pea beans, you can substitute them with French or even runner beans if you prefer.

Note: Be careful when handling chillies as they will irritate the skin and eyes. Wear thin rubber gloves and be careful not to touch your eyes. Or wash your hands thoroughly afterwards.

Serves 4
Preparation and cooking time: 25 minutes
(plus marinating time)

Stir-Fry Sauce: In a small bowl or cup combine ¼ cup chicken stock, 1 tbsp grated palm or soft brown sugar, 2 tbsp fish sauce. Stir until the sugar dissolves and set aside.

450 g (1 lb) pork fillet, trimmed and sliced into strips
1 tbsp red curry paste (page 44)
2 tbsp oil
2 cloves garlic, finely sliced
1 cup green beans, sliced into 2.5 cm (1 inch) lengths
3 kaffir lime leaves or 1 tsp grated lime zest
1–2 red chillies, finely sliced

To serve: rice, fish sauce, chilli sauce or sliced chillies and lime wedges

- Combine the pork and curry paste and set aside for 15 minutes to marinate if time allows.

- Heat a wok or large deep frying pan on high until smoking and add the oil. Swirl the oil around to coat the wok or pan and heat for a few more seconds.

- Add the pork and garlic, and stir-fry for 2–3 minutes or until the pork begins to colour.

- Add the beans, lime leaves and chilli and stir-fry for 3–4 minutes, adding a little water or stock to avoid burning.

- Stir through the prepared sauce and stir-fry for a further 2 minutes on medium heat.

- Turn off the heat and do the taste test. Add fish sauce, sugar or chilli as desired.

GARLIC PRAWN AND SNOW PEA STIR-FRY

This must be the quickest and easiest recipe in the book, particularly if you buy shelled prawns. It takes just a few minutes but produces a tasty and nutritious meal that will impress family and friends.

Note: Be careful when handling chillies as they will irritate the skin and eyes. Wear thin rubber gloves and be careful not to touch your eyes. Or wash your hands thoroughly afterwards.

Serves 4
Preparation and cooking time: 20 minutes

Stir-Fry Sauce: In a small bowl or cup combine ¼ cup chicken or fish stock, 1 tbsp fish sauce, 2 tsp grated palm or soft brown sugar, 2 tbsp lime juice and 1 tbsp oyster sauce. Stir until the sugar dissolves and set aside.

2 tbsp oil
1 tbsp finely chopped garlic
20–24 king prawns (or equivalent weight smaller prawns),
**   shelled with tails intact**
300 g (10 oz) snow peas (mangetout), trimmed
1–2 red chillies, sliced
¼ cup coriander leaves (optional)

To serve: rice, fish sauce, chilli sauce or sliced chillies and
**   lime wedges**

- Heat a wok or large deep frying pan on high until smoking and add the oil. Swirl the oil around to coat the wok or pan and heat for a few more seconds.

- Add the garlic, stir once and add the prawns. Stir-fry for 2–3 minutes, taking care not to over cook.

- Add the snow peas and chillies with a splash of water or stock and stir-fry for a minute or so until they turn bright green.

- Add the stir-fry sauce and heat through for a further minute. Turn off the heat and do the taste test. Add fish sauce or lime juice as desired.

- Serve sprinkled with the coriander leaves if using.

HOT AND SPICY SEAFOOD STIR-FRY

This is a sumptuous seafood feast with tantalizingly spicy flavours and fresh herb aromas. Use the freshest seafood you can get for this delicious dish.

Serves 4
Preparation and cooking time: 30 minutes

Stir-Fry Sauce: In a small bowl or cup combine 2 tbsp fish sauce, 2 tbsp lime juice and 2 tsp grated palm or soft brown sugar. Stir until the sugar dissolves and set aside.

Oil for deep frying
2 small fillets white fish
2 tbsp oil
2 shallots, finely sliced
2 tbsp roast chilli paste (page 52)
2 tbsp finely sliced lemongrass, white part only
6 kaffir lime leaves or 2 tsp grated lime zest
1 tbsp sliced galangal or ginger
8 king prawns, shelled
8 pieces squid
8 scallops
¼ cup chicken or fish stock
3–4 dried red chillies, crushed

To serve: rice, fish sauce, chilli sauce or sliced chillies and lime wedges

- Heat the oil for deep frying and fry the fish fillets until golden. Drain and slice each fillet into chunks. Keep warm.

- Heat the 2 tbsp of oil in a wok or large pan over high heat and fry the shallots for a minute.

- Turn down the heat a little and add the chilli paste, lemongrass, lime leaves and galangal and stir-fry for a minute or so until fragrant.

- Add the prawns and squid and stir-fry for 2–3 minutes. Add the scallops, stock and stir-fry sauce, turn up the heat and cook for a further minute or two, or until the seafood is cooked.

- Toss through the cooked fish and chillies. Turn off the heat and do the taste test. Add fish sauce, sugar or chilli as desired.

- Serve.

MIXED VEGETABLE STIR-FRY

This is no ordinary vegetarian dish. With heaps of delicious, spicy veggies topped with roasted sunflower and sesame seeds, this stir-fry is too good to keep just for the vegetarians.

Note: Be careful when handling chillies as they will irritate the skin and eyes. Wear thin rubber gloves and be careful not to touch your eyes. Or wash your hands thoroughly afterwards.

Serves 4
Preparation and cooking time: 40 minutes

Stir-Fry Sauce: In a small bowl or cup combine ¼ cup vegetable stock or water, 2 tbsp soy sauce, 2 tbsp fish sauce, 2 tbsp lime juice, 2 tsp hot chilli sauce, ½ tsp freshly ground black pepper, 1 tsp grated palm or soft brown sugar, 2 tsp cornflour dissolved in 2 tbsp water. Stir until the sugar dissolves and set aside.

2 medium potatoes, peeled
2 carrots, peeled
2 tbsp oil
1 onion, sliced
4 cloves garlic, finely sliced
6 fresh or dried (and soaked) shitake mushrooms, sliced
1 cup straw or button mushrooms, sliced
1 cup shredded pak choi/bok choy
2 tbsp toasted sunflower seeds
2 tbsp coarsely chopped, roasted cashew nuts
1 tsp toasted black sesame seeds
2 long red chillies, sliced
A few basil leaves for garnish (optional)

To serve: rice, fish sauce, chilli sauce or sliced chillies and
    lime wedges

- Julienne or grate the potatoes and carrots into thin strips. Cook in boiling salted water for about 3 minutes or until just cooked. Plunge into cold water. Drain and set aside.

- Heat the wok or large pan over high heat until smoking. Add the oil and swirl to coat.

- Add the onion and garlic and stir-fry for a minute.

- Add all the vegetables and a splash of water or stock and stir-fry for 2–3 minutes or until the pak choi has softened and turned bright green.

- Add the prepared sauce and stir-fry over high heat for a further minute or until the sauce cooks and thickens.

- Turn off the heat and do the taste test. Add fish sauce, sugar or lime juice as desired.

- Transfer to a serving dish and scatter over the seeds, cashews, sliced chillies and basil leaves (if using) and serve.

PERFECT PAD THAI

Pad Thai, probably the best known of all Thai dishes, is the bringing together of many different ingredients into a sensational harmony of sweet, sour, hot and salty flavours that are the foundations of Thai cuisine.

The ultimate street food, Pad Thai in various forms is readily available on the ubiquitous street stalls, cafés and casual eateries around Thailand and is a very popular dish with locals and tourists alike. The best Pad Thai, as eaten and loved by countless Thais, is a light, relatively dry dish with fresh and complex flavours and is quite at odds with the western version which tends to be rather heavy and oily. By making Pad Thai at home you decide what goes into it and the amount of oil used, so you can create the dish exactly to your tastes.

Making traditional Pad Thai at home can appear to be a bit daunting, particularly if you cannot get some of the ingredients, but with proper preparation Pad Thai is not difficult. In addition to some modified recipes, the step by step guide and tips below will help make creating your own delicious Pad Thai easy and fun.

Tips for the Perfect Pad Thai
Preparation, Preparation, Preparation!

- Prepare the Pad Thai sauce (page 54) well beforehand and have it ready to use.

- Have all the other ingredients, such as lime juice, peanuts and coriander, at the ready in small dishes laid out in the kitchen in the order that you will use them.

- Prepare all the vegetables and any meat or fish that you would like to use.

- Prepare the noodles so that they are ready to add to the wok or pan.

- Do not over cook the noodles – perfectly cooked noodles should be slightly chewy. Follow the instructions on the packet as cooking times vary slightly from brand to brand.

- Familiarize yourself with all the steps before you start.

- Using two wooden spoons to toss and stir the ingredients is easier and more effective than using one.

Two other really important points

1. Start with a hot, well oiled wok or pan.

2. Cook your Pad Thai in one or two serves only; too much food in the wok will stew rather than stir-fry and you won't get that lovely 'wok' flavour.

BANGKOK STYLE PAD THAI

This is a wonderful dish, non-oily, light and brimming with delicious complex flavours. This recipe is based on the Pad Thai found at the popular street stalls in Bangkok where some of the best Thai food is prepared and sold.

Remember to have all the ingredients prepared and ready to go in the order that you will need them.

Makes enough for 2 small servings
Preparation time: 20 minutes.
Cooking time: 4–5 minutes

120 g (4 oz) thin rice noodles
2–3 tbsp oil
60 g (2 oz) firm tofu, diced
1 shallot or ½ onion, finely chopped
2–3 cloves garlic, finely chopped
1 tsp shrimp paste (optional)
200 g (7 oz) small prawns, shelled
¾ cup Pad Thai sauce (page 54), warmed
1 egg, beaten
1 tbsp roasted peanuts, finely chopped
1 cup bean sprouts
2 tsp thinly sliced pickled radish or turnip (optional)
½ tsp ground white pepper
30 g (1 oz) garlic chives or spring onion, sliced

To serve: white vinegar or lime wedges, fish sauce, sliced red
or green chillies, white sugar, chopped roasted peanuts

- Soak the noodles in hot water for about 10 minutes (or according to the packet instructions) until limp but still firm to the touch. Rinse under cold water and drain.

- Heat a wok or large pan until very hot and just starting to smoke. Add 2 tablespoons of oil, swirl it around and add the tofu, onion and garlic. Stir-fry for about a minute and add the shrimp paste. Stir for a few seconds until it breaks down a little.

- Add the prawns and stir-fry for about a minute or until pink and almost cooked.

- Add the noodles and about half the Pad Thai sauce. Toss and stir-fry vigorously for about a minute or until the noodles are separated and soft enough to be eaten but still al dente. Sprinkle on a little water if the noodles need to be softened a bit more.

- Move the noodles to the edges of the wok. Sprinkle a little more oil into the middle of wok/pan and add the egg. Stir it around for about 15 seconds until set and then bring everything back together.

- Add half the remaining Pad Thai sauce, peanuts, bean sprouts, pickled radish or turnip if using, and pepper. Continue to toss and move the ingredients around in the wok/pan until the prawns are cooked and everything is well combined.

- Stir in the garlic chives or spring onion, take off the heat and do the taste test. Add more Pad Thai sauce if you want a stronger taste, return to the heat and toss through. Serve immediately.

EASY PRAWN PAD THAI

This is an easy but very tasty recipe that needs just a handful of ingredients and the Pad Thai sauce. You can add some diced tofu with the prawns if you happen to have some.

Makes enough for 2 small servings
Preparation and cooking time: 20 minutes

120 g (4 oz) thin rice noodles
2–3 tbsp oil
120 g (4 oz) large peeled prawns
2–3 cloves garlic, finely chopped
¼ cup Pad Thai sauce (page 54), warmed
2 eggs, beaten
2 cups bean sprouts
2 spring onions, sliced

To serve: white vinegar or lime wedges, fish sauce, sliced red or green chillies, white sugar, chopped roasted peanuts

- Soak the noodles in hot water for about 10 minutes (or according to the packet instructions) until limp but still firm to the touch. Rinse under cold water and drain.

- Heat a wok or large pan until very hot and just starting to smoke. Add the oil and swirl it around until it coats the sides. Add the prawns and garlic and stir-fry for 2 minutes or until the prawns are cooked.

- Add the noodles and about three-quarters of the Pad Thai sauce and stir and toss until the noodles are separated and soft enough to eat but still al dente. Add a splash of water if required.

- Move the noodle mixture to the edges of the wok, sprinkle a little oil into the middle and pour in the egg. Stir it around for a few seconds until set and bring everything back together again.

- Add the bean sprouts and spring onions and toss and stir-fry for a further minute or so until they mixed through.

- Take off the heat and do the taste test. Add a little more Pad Thai sauce if required, return to the heat and toss through.

- Serve immediately.

QUICK CHICKEN PAD THAI

A very tasty and satisfying dish for Pad Thai fans that is also really easy
to prepare. The chicken can be marinated several hours beforehand and
refrigerated until required. Remove from the fridge about 30 minutes
before using to bring it to room temperature.

Makes enough for 2 small servings
Preparation and cooking time: 25 minutes

1 level tsp cornflour
1 tbsp soy sauce
200 g (6 oz) thinly sliced chicken
120 g (4 oz) thin rice noodles
2–3 tbsp oil
2–3 cloves garlic, finely sliced
¾ cup Pad Thai sauce (page 54), warmed
1 egg, lightly beaten
2 cups bean sprouts
2 spring onions, sliced

To serve: white vinegar or lime wedges, fish sauce, sliced red
   or green chillies, white sugar, chopped roasted peanuts

- In a medium bowl, dissolve the cornflour with the soy sauce. Add the chicken and mix well. Cover and set aside.

- Soak the noodles in hot water for about 10 minutes (or according to the packet instructions) until limp but still firm to the touch. Rinse under cold water and drain.

- Heat a wok or large pan until very hot and just starting to smoke. Add about 2 tbsp of the oil and swirl it around to coat the sides and add the garlic and chicken. Stir-fry for 4–5 minutes until cooked through. Add a little more oil during cooking if the wok/pan dries out too much.

- Add the noodles and about three-quarters of the Pad Thai sauce and stir and toss until the noodles are separated and soft enough to eat but still al dente. Add a splash of water if required.

- Move the noodle mixture to the edges of the wok, sprinkle a little more oil into the middle and pour in the egg. Stir it around for a few seconds until set and bring everything together again.

- Add the bean sprouts and spring onions and stir-fry for a further minute or so until they are well mixed through.

- Take off the heat and do the taste test. Add a little more Pad Thai sauce if required, return to the heat and toss through.

- Serve immediately.

SIMPLE SOUPS

Unlike the thick, rich soups common in the west, Thai soups tend to be clear, thin and spicy – the best example of which is the world famous Tom Yum Soup – although some are made with the addition of coconut milk. In Thailand soups are generally eaten as part of the main course with rice or noodles, but in small servings they make delicious starters to a western style meal.

Really good, tasty chicken stock is essential for many of these soups, so if you have time, make your own. See the recipe on page 99.

THAI CHICKEN SOUP IN COCONUT MILK

A very easy yet incredibly satisfying soup that can also be served with stir-fried vegetables and rice for a complete meal. The dried, ground ginger gives the soup a richer flavour.

Serves 3–4
Preparation and cooking time: 30 minutes

1 cup chicken stock (page 99)
1 tbsp finely sliced lemongrass (fresh or frozen), white part only
1 tsp dried ground ginger
1 tsp grated fresh galangal or ginger
1 clove garlic, finely sliced
1 tsp tamarind paste
1 tsp grated palm or soft brown sugar
350 g (12 oz) sliced chicken breast or thigh fillets
1 x 400 g (14 oz) can coconut milk
2–3 small red chillies, sliced (see page 134)
1 tbsp fish sauce
1 tsp light soy sauce
1 large red chilli, sliced into strips (optional)

- Bring the chicken stock to the boil over high heat in a medium sized saucepan. Add the lemongrass, dried and fresh ginger, garlic, tamarind and sugar and simmer for about 3 minutes to bring out the flavour.

- Add the chicken to the simmering stock, bring back to the boil and simmer gently for 7–8 minutes until cooked through.

- Stir in the coconut milk and bring back to the boil and simmer for a further 3 minutes.

- Stir through the chillies, fish sauce and soy sauce and heat for a minute.

- Turn off the heat and do the taste test. Add more fish sauce, soy sauce or chilli as desired.

- Serve garnished with strips of chilli if using.

TOM YUM GOONG

This wonderful clear soup, generously flavoured with fresh herbs and chillies, is famous around the world for its delicious hot and sour flavours. The fresh prawns can be substituted with chunks of white fish (*Tom Yum Pla*) or chicken (*Tom Yum Gai*) if preferred.

The fresher the ingredients, the better this soup will be.

Note: Be careful when handling chillies as they will irritate the skin and eyes. Wear thin rubber gloves and be careful not to touch your eyes. Or wash your hands thoroughly afterwards.

Serves 4
Preparation and cooking time: 30 minutes

2 cups chicken stock (page 99)
2 stalks fresh lemongrass, white part only (or use equivalent amount of frozen)
2.5 cm (1 inch) piece galangal or ginger, peeled and finely sliced
4 kaffir lime leaves shredded or 1 tsp grated lime zest
1 tbsp tamarind paste
2 tbsp roast chilli paste (page 52)
16 king prawns, shelled (or equivalent amount of smaller prawns)
1 x 450 g (16 oz) can straw mushrooms
1 ripe tomato, sliced into thin wedges
2 green chillies, seeded and thinly sliced
Juice of 1 lime
1 tbsp fish sauce
½ cup coriander leaves

- Bring the stock and 2 cups of water to the boil over high heat in a medium-sized saucepan. Turn down to a simmer.

- Meanwhile, slice off the roots from the lemongrass stalks and crush the stems with the side of the knife. Slice thinly.

- Add the lemongrass, galangal (or ginger), kaffir lime leaves (or zest) and tamarind to the simmering water. Stir and simmer for 4–5 minutes to bring out the flavour.

- Stir in the roasted chilli paste and bring back to a simmer. Add the prawns and straw mushrooms and bring to the boil. Simmer for about 5 minutes or until the prawns are cooked.

- Add the tomato and chillies. Turn off the heat and stir in the lime juice, fish sauce and half the coriander. Do the taste test and add more fish sauce or lime juice if desired.

- Serve in individual bowls, garnished with the remaining coriander.

THAI CHICKEN NOODLE SOUP

The original in comfort food, this delicious soup is perfect for nursing a cold, tired body on a chilly winter's day. If you have some home-made, real chicken stock you can make a perfect soup in minutes.

Note: Be careful when handling chillies as they will irritate the skin and eyes. Wear thin rubber gloves and be careful not to touch your eyes. Or wash your hands thoroughly afterwards.

Serves 4–6
Preparation and cooking time: 30 minutes

240 g (8 oz) dried rice noodles (thick or thin)
1 tbsp oil
2 cloves garlic, thinly sliced
2 red chillies, de-seeded, finely chopped
1 tbsp sliced lemongrass (fresh or frozen), white part only
1½ litres (6 cups/3.3 pints) chicken stock (page 99)
450 g (1 lb) chicken breast fillets, trimmed
2 tsp roast chilli paste (page 52)
80 ml (⅓ cup) fresh lime juice
2 tbsp fish sauce
1 cup baby spinach leaves
1 tbsp crispy fried onion (optional)

To serve: soy sauce, lime wedges, sliced red chilli

- Soak the noodles in hot water for about 10 minutes (or according to the packet instructions). Drain and set aside.

- Meanwhile, heat the oil in a large saucepan over medium-high heat. Add the garlic, chillies and lemongrass, and cook, stirring, for 2 minutes or until fragrant.

- Add the stock and bring to the boil. Add the chicken and reduce the heat to very low. Simmer, covered, for 15 minutes or until cooked through.

- Transfer the chicken to a plate. Set aside for 5 minutes to cool slightly and coarsely shred.

- Stir the chilli paste into the stock and add the lime juice, fish sauce and shredded chicken, and cook for a further minute or until heated through.

- Turn off the heat and do the taste test. Add more fish sauce, lime juice or chilli as desired.

- Divide the noodles among 4 deep bowls, top with the spinach leaves and ladle the soup over.

- Top with the crispy fried onion if using and serve.

THAI RICE SOUP

In Thailand, this type of soup is a staple for breakfast and is often made from leftover ingredients from the previous night's meal. Along with the rice, it can therefore contain almost anything – vegetables, fish, meat, tofu or a combination of these. It is a very easy soup to make and a good use of leftovers, so use whatever you have in the fridge.

Serves 3–4
Preparation and cooking time: 20 minutes

3 cups vegetable or chicken stock (page 99)
2 tsp grated galangal or ginger
1 small onion, finely sliced
1 tbsp sliced lemongrass, white part only
1 carrot, sliced
½ cup sliced greens (pak choi/bok choy, spinach,
    cabbage, mustard greens)
2 cups cooked rice
1 cup diced cooked chicken, pork or beef
2 tsp roast chilli paste (page 52)
1 tbsp fish sauce
1 spring onion, sliced
½ cup coriander leaves

To serve: soy sauce, hot sauce, lime wedges

- Bring the stock and 1 cup of water to the boil. Lower the heat and add the galangal (or ginger), onion, lemongrass and carrot. Simmer for 5 minutes.

- Add the greens and simmer for 3–4 minutes. Stir in all the remaining ingredients except for the spring onion and coriander and simmer for a further 5 minutes until everything is well heated through.

- Stir in the spring onion and coriander and serve.

Tasty Vegetable Stock – *Makes about 1.5 litres (3.3 pints) and freezes well for up to 3 months. You will need a large stock pot or saucepan.*

1 tbsp olive oil
2 onions, roughly chopped
3 sticks celery, roughly chopped
2 carrots, roughly chopped
1 swede, peeled and roughly chopped
3 litres (7 pints) water
1 tsp black peppercorns
3 bay leaves
6 fresh parsley stalks

Heat the oil in a stock pan and add the onions, celery, carrots and swede. Stir-fry for about 5 minutes until lightly browned. Add the water, peppercorns, bay leaves and parsley stalks. Bring to the boil and simmer very gently for about 2 hours. Skim the top now and again. Cool the stock and strain through a fine strainer into a clean container. Cover and store in the fridge and use as required or freeze.

GLASS NOODLE SOUP

This light, gently flavoured, nutritious soup made with mung bean noodles is a traditional cooling accompaniment to spicy dishes. It's also wonderful when you want something soothing and comforting, particularly if you use home-made, real chicken stock.

Serves 3–4
Preparation and cooking time: 25 minutes

60 g (2 oz) dried glass noodles
1 tsp soy sauce
120 g (4 oz) minced pork
1 tbsp oil
1 spring onion, white and green parts separated and sliced
4 cloves garlic, crushed
1 litre (4 cups/2.2 pints) chicken stock (page 99)
½ tsp freshly ground white or black pepper
¼ tsp sugar
1 tbsp fish sauce
1 tbsp coriander leaves

- Soak the noodles in warm water for about 10 minutes to soften (or according to the packet instructions), drain and set aside.

- Meanwhile, mix the soy sauce into the meat and form into small meatballs, about the size of a marble.

- Heat the oil in a medium saucepan and fry the white part of the spring onion and garlic for a few seconds. Do not allow to colour. Add the stock, pepper and sugar and bring to the boil. Add the meatballs and simmer for 2–3 minutes.

- Add the noodles and simmer for a further 2 minutes. Stir in the fish sauce and the remaining green part of the spring onion.

- Turn off the heat and do the taste test. Add more fish sauce as desired. Serve garnished with the coriander.

THAI PUMPKIN SOUP

This is a deliciously warming, velvety soup that can be made as mild or as spicy as you like. I like it fairly mild to allow the sweetness of the pumpkin to shine through, so add a little chilli to the recipe if you want it hotter.

Serves 4
Preparation and cooking time: 45 minutes

1.5 kg (3.3 lb) pumpkin
1 tbsp oil
2 tbsp yellow curry paste
1 litre (4 cups/2.2 pints) chicken stock (page 99)
1 cup coconut cream
1 tbsp fish sauce
1 tbsp coriander leaves, chopped

- Peel the pumpkin, remove the pith and seeds and slice into smallish chunks.

- Heat the oil in a saucepan on medium heat and fry the curry paste for 2 minutes or until fragrant.

- Add the pumpkin and stock and bring to the boil. Simmer for about 20 minutes or until the pumpkin is very soft.

- Purée using a stick or jug blender until smooth. Stir in the coconut cream and fish sauce and heat through.

- Serve garnished with the coriander.

THAI LEMONGRASS SOUP

A delicious and aromatic soup that is an elegant starter or, with the addition of prawns or chicken, a more substantial dish that can be part of the main meal. As with most soups, use whatever vegetables are in season. This is really simple and quick to make.

The lemongrass is not meant to be eaten.

Serves 4
Preparation and cooking time: 20 minutes

3 stalks fresh lemongrass, white part only (or equivalent amount of frozen)
1½ litres (6 cups/3.3 pints) chicken stock (page 99)
2 tsp grated galangal or ginger
1 small onion, finely chopped
6 white or black peppercorns, crushed
120 g (4 oz) button mushrooms, sliced
1 red or green capsicum, thinly sliced
½ cup sliced bamboo shoots
1 tbsp fish sauce
½ cup coriander leaves

- Crush the lemongrass stalks with the back of a large knife, and slice into 2.5 cm (1 inch) pieces.

- Bring the stock to a simmer in a large saucepan and add the lemongrass, galangal (or ginger), onion and peppercorns. Simmer for 5 minutes.

- Add the mushrooms, capsicum and bamboo shoots and simmer for a further 5 minutes.

- Stir in the fish sauce and coriander. Serve.

SWEET POTATO, COCONUT AND LIME SOUP

This smooth, spicy soup is easy to make and very, very tasty.

Note: Be careful when handling the chilli (if used) as it will irritate the skin and eyes. See page 136.

Serves 4–5
Preparation and cooking time: 40 minutes

1 tbsp oil
1 onion, sliced
1 tbsp red curry paste (page 44)
2 tsp grated galangal or ginger
500 g (1.1 lb) sweet potato, peeled and diced
500 ml (2 cups/1.1 pints) vegetable stock
1 x 400 ml (14 fl oz) can coconut milk
1 tbsp fish sauce
1 tsp grated lime zest
2 tbsp lime juice
1 red chilli, de-seeded and finely chopped (optional)
1 tbsp chopped coriander

- Heat the oil in a large saucepan and fry the onion for about 3 minutes until soft.

- Add the curry paste and galangal (or ginger) and fry for a further 2 minutes until aromatic.

- Add the sweet potato, stir-fry for a minute and stir in the stock. Bring to the boil and simmer for 15 minutes or until the potato is very tender.

- Purée with a stick or jug blender until smooth and add all the remaining ingredients except the chilli and coriander. Simmer gently for about 5 minutes until heated through.

- Turn off the heat and do the taste test. Add more fish sauce or lime juice as desired.

- Stir through the chilli if using and serve garnished with the coriander.

EASY VEGETABLE SIDE DISHES

A wide variety of vegetables may be used to make fresh, healthy side dishes to accompany meat or fish based Thai dishes. Chinese greens, such as pak choi are good on their own, as is asparagus, broccolini, green beans and aubergine, but a mix of fresh, colourful vegetables in one dish is also delicious. So experiment with good quality, seasonal vegetables. You really can't go too far wrong.

PAK CHOI WITH GARLIC AND GINGER

This is a delicious and healthy side dish that is a synch to make and absolutely wonderful with a meat, fish or chicken based main dish. Or add some tofu, chicken or seafood if you want a quick and healthy meal.

Note: Be careful when handling the chilli (if used) as it will irritate the skin and eyes. See page 136.

Serves 4–6 (as a side dish)
Preparation and cooking time: 15 minutes

Stir-Fry Sauce: In a small bowl or cup combine 2 tbsp soy, 2 tbsp fish sauce, 2 tbsp oyster sauce, 1 tbsp sweet chilli sauce, 2 tsp grated palm or soft brown sugar and 2 tsp lime juice. Stir until the sugar dissolves and set aside.

6 heads pak choi/bok choy
2 tbsp oil
4 cloves garlic, finely sliced
1 tbsp grated ginger
1 red chilli, finely sliced (optional)

- Separate the pak choi leaves, rinse and slice off the white stems. Slice the stems lengthways into two or three pieces depending on how wide they are.

- Heat a wok or large pan over medium to high heat and add the oil. Swirl to coat, add the garlic and ginger and stir-fry for a few seconds. Do not let the garlic colour.

- Add the sliced stems and a splash of water and stir-fry for 2 minutes. Add the leaves and about 2 tablespoons of the stir-fry sauce and stir-fry for a minute or two.

- Add another 2–3 tablespoons of the sauce and stir-fry for a further 2–3 minutes or until the pak choi is bright green. The stems should have softened but should still be crunchy.

- Turn off the heat and do the taste test. Add fish sauce, sugar, lime juice or chilli as desired.

MIXED VEGETABLES WITH LEMONGRASS

This is a really tasty way of eating all those fresh summer vegetables – be sure to use whatever is fresh and in season. Add a little protein in the way of tofu, chicken, pork, beef or seafood and you have a complete meal in very little time.

To ensure that some of the vegetables don't end up overcooked, always start by adding the firmer vegetables, like carrots, that take longer to cook, adding those that cook quickly (such as snow peas/mangetout) towards the end.

Serves 4–6 (as a side dish)
Preparation and cooking time: 30 minutes

Stir-Fry Sauce: In a small bowl or cup combine 2 tbsp fish sauce, 1 tbsp soy sauce, 1 tbsp lime juice, 1 tbsp sweet chilli sauce, and 1 tsp cornflour mixed with 4 tbsp chicken or vegetable stock.

2 tbsp oil
4 cloves garlic, finely sliced
1 tbsp grated galangal or ginger
2 tbsp finely sliced lemongrass (fresh or frozen), white part only
1 carrot, peeled and thinly sliced
1 small red capsicum, cut into small chunks
1 small green capsicum, cut into small chunks
1 cup broccoli florets
½ cup mushrooms, sliced
2 spring onions, sliced into 2.5 cm (1 inch) lengths
1 cup snow peas (mangetout), topped and tailed

- Heat a wok or large pan over medium to high heat and add the oil. Swirl to coat, add the garlic and galangal (or ginger) and stir-fry for a minute.

- Add the lemongrass and carrot and a splash of water and stir-fry for 2 minutes.

- Add the capsicums, broccoli and mushrooms, with another splash of water, and stir-fry for a further 2–3 minutes until the broccoli is a bright green and starting to soften a little.

- Stir in the spring onions and snow peas/mangetout, stir-fry for a minute and add the prepared sauce. Stir until thickened. This will take only a few seconds.

- Turn off the heat and do the taste test. Add fish or soy sauce, sweet chilli sauce or lime juice as desired.

CHILLI AND GARLIC BROCCOLINI

A cross between broccoli and the Chinese 'gai-lan', the slim, elegant stems and smaller flower heads of broccolini are ideal for quick and easy stir-fries that are tasty and nutritious too. Broccoli cut into small florets is a good substitute or try this recipe with asparagus when it's in season.

Serves 4–6 (as a side dish)
Preparation and cooking time: 15 minutes

Stir-Fry Sauce: In a small bowl or cup combine 3 tbsp fish sauce, 1 tbsp lime juice, 2 tsp grated palm or soft brown sugar and 3 tbsp warm water. Stir until the sugar dissolves and set aside.

1 tbsp oil
6–8 cloves garlic, finely chopped
1 tsp chilli flakes
2 bunches broccolini, trimmed

- Heat a wok or pan over medium-high heat, add the oil and swirl to coat. Add the garlic and stir-fry for a minute.

- Stir in the chilli flakes followed by the broccolini and about two-thirds of the prepared sauce.

- Stir-fry for 3–4 minutes or until the broccolini is tender crisp. Add a splash of water if the wok/pan dries out before the broccolini is cooked.

- Remove from the heat and do the taste test. Add more of the prepared sauce if desired.

SWEET AND SOUR AUBERGINE WITH BASIL

The secret of this delicious, flavour packed dish is to use the freshest, tastiest aubergine you can get. Any variety will do but it works really well with the large, plump purple ones. Or try it with white for an interesting change.

Note: Be careful when handling chillies (see page 136).

Serves 4 (as a side dish)
Preparation and cooking time: 20 minutes

Stir-Fry Sauce: In a small bowl or cup combine 3 tbsp lime juice, 2 tbsp fish sauce and 1 tbsp grated palm or soft brown sugar. Stir until the sugar dissolves and set aside.

2 tbsp oil
2 cloves garlic, finely sliced
1–2 hot red chillies, finely sliced
1 large (or equivalent quantity smaller) aubergine, sliced into small chunks
1 cup Thai or sweet basil leaves

- Heat a wok or large pan over medium to high heat and add the oil. Swirl to coat and add the garlic and chillies. Stir-fry for a minute or so until the garlic starts to colour.

- Add the aubergine and stir until well coated with the oil mixture. Stir in 1 cup of water, bring to the boil and turn down the heat a little.

- Cover the wok/pan with a lid and cook the aubergine for 5–6 minutes, stirring once or twice, until it softens and the water completely evaporates. Add a little more water during that time if the wok/pan dries out before the aubergine is soft.

- Add the prepared sauce and stir-fry for a few seconds until the liquid evaporates.

- Stir in the basil and remove from the heat. Do the taste test and add fish sauce, lime juice or sugar as required.

RICE DISHES

Rice is the staple food of Thailand as of most Asian countries. A typical Thai meal consists of a dish of steamed jasmine rice accompanied by other dishes such as stir-fries, curries and soups. Fine, medium grained and naturally sweet smelling jasmine rice is indigenous to Thailand and grows in abundance in the paddy fields of Thailand's central plains. Because of its natural fragrance and to balance the aromatic, pungent flavours of the dishes that it is served with, jasmine rice is usually served simply steamed.

Sticky rice, also called glutinous rice, is a unique type of rice popular in northern Thailand. The unusually high level of starches present in the grains of this rice variety gives it a sticky texture when cooked. Sticky rice is often used for sweet dishes in western Thai restaurants.

STEAMED JASMINE RICE

The secret of perfectly steamed jasmine rice lies in the quantity of water used. Too little and the rice will not cook properly, too much and it will be soggy. The following recipe will ensure perfect results every time.

Serves 4–5
Preparation and cooking time: 20 minutes

2½ cups Thai jasmine rice
3 cups water

- Place the rice in a smallish, heavy based saucepan with a tight-fitting lid (capacity of about 2 litres/4½ pints). Cover with plenty of cold water, stir and drain. Repeat twice more. This helps remove excess starch and broken rice grains, both of which can make the rice mushy.

- Add the 3 cups of water, cover the saucepan and bring to the boil over medium heat.

- Stir, turn the heat down to as low as you can and cover the saucepan again. Cook for about 10 minutes or until all the water has evaporated.

- Turn off the heat and let the rice stand for a further 5 minutes. Serve hot.

STIR-FRIED RICE WITH CHICKEN

Thais typically cook more rice than can be eaten at one meal. Leftover rice is never thrown away. Instead it is combined with other ingredients and turned into tasty stir-fried rice dishes.

This is a really simple recipe that makes handy work of leftover rice and cooked chicken. Take both out of the fridge about 30 minutes beforehand to allow them to come to room temperature. If you want to make this dish and don't have leftovers, follow the recipe for Steamed Jasmine Rice (page 151) and stir-fry some chicken strips in a little oil for 4–5 minutes until cooked through.

Note: Be careful when handling the chilli as it will irritate the skin and eyes. Wear thin rubber gloves and be careful not to touch your eyes. Or wash your hands thoroughly afterwards.

Serves 2–3
Preparation and cooking time: 25 minutes

Stir-Fry Sauce: In a small bowl or cup combine 1 tbsp fish sauce, 2 tsp light soy sauce, 1 tsp grated palm or soft brown sugar, 2 tsp hot chilli sauce and ½ tsp ground black pepper.

2 tbsp oil
1 egg, lightly beaten
2 cloves garlic, finely sliced
4 cups steamed jasmine rice
1 cup cooked chicken, sliced into bite sized pieces
2 spring onions, sliced into 2.5 cm (1 inch) lengths
5 cm (2 inch) piece cucumber, thinly sliced
1 long red chilli, sliced
1 lime, quartered

- Heat a wok or large pan over high heat, add 2 tsp of the oil and swirl it round to coat the surface.

- Add the beaten egg and swirl around the wok/pan so that you have a thinnish layer of egg. Cook until set.

- Remove the egg and slice into strips. Set aside.

- Heat the remaining oil to the wok/pan and add the garlic. Stir-fry for 30 seconds.

- Add the rice and gently stir and break up any lumps. Add the chicken, spring onions, strips of egg and prepared sauce and stir-fry for 3–4 minutes until well heated through and the rice grains are separate.

- Turn off the heat and do the taste test. Add fish sauce, or chilli sauce as desired.

- Serve garnished with the sliced cucumber, chilli, lime wedges to squeeze over the top and extra soy sauce.

PORK AND PRAWN FRIED RICE

A mild tasting and substantial dish, this is one the whole family can enjoy. It's quick and simple to make and you can make it even quicker by substituting cooked chicken for the pork in this recipe. Serve it with hot sauce for the chilli lovers.

Serves 4
Preparation and cooking time: 35 minutes

120 g (4 oz) thinly sliced pork
4 tbsp light soy sauce
4 tbsp oil
4 eggs, beaten
1 onion, finely sliced
2 cloves garlic, finely chopped
120 g (4 oz) prawns, shelled and de-veined
4 cups steamed jasmine rice
2 tbsp sweet chilli sauce
1 tbsp palm or soft brown sugar
2 spring onions, sliced into 2.5 cm (1 inch) pieces
Lime wedges to serve

- Combine the pork with 1 tbsp of the soy sauce and set aside, while preparing the remaining ingredients.

- Heat 1 tablespoon of the oil in a wok or large pan over high heat and swirl it round to coat the surface.

- Add the beaten egg and swirl around the wok/pan so that you have a thinnish layer of egg. Cook until set.

- Remove the egg and slice into strips. Set aside.

- Heat the remaining oil in the same wok/pan over medium heat and fry the onion for 2–3 minutes or until soft.

- Add the garlic and fry for a few seconds until aromatic. Add the pork and stir-fry for 2 minutes.

- Stir in the prawns and cook for a further 2 minutes or until the pork and prawns are cooked.

- Add all the remaining ingredients (except the lime wedges) and stir-fry until combined and hot.

- Serve with some lime wedges.

COCONUT RICE

This is a really flavoursome but easy to prepare rice dish for those times when you want to add an extra touch to a special occasion.

Note: The coconut milk has a tendency to stick to the bottom of the pan and burn, so you will need to keep a close eye on this whilst cooking.

Serves 4
Preparation and cooking time: 25 minutes

2 cups jasmine rice
2 cups coconut milk
1¾ cups water
½ tsp sugar
1–2 tbsp toasted coconut flakes (optional)

- Place the rice in a smallish, heavy based saucepan with a tight-fitting lid (capacity of about 2 litres/4½ pints). Cover with plenty of cold water, stir and drain. Repeat twice more.

- Add the coconut milk, water and sugar, place on medium heat and bring to the boil, stirring often.

- Turn the heat down to low, partly cover the pan and cook, stirring now and again, for 10–12 minutes until all the liquid has evaporated.

- Turn the heat off but leave the pan on the stove. Cover tightly and let the rice stand for at least 10 minutes.

- Fluff up lightly with a fork and serve sprinkled with coconut flakes if using.

BASIL AND PRAWN FRIED RICE

Traditionally, this is a really hot and garlicky dish, delicious for the chilli tolerant. I have toned down the chillies and garlic a little to cater for western tastebuds, but it is still a great taste for spice lovers.

Note: Be careful when handling chillies as they will irritate the skin and eyes. Wear thin rubber gloves and be careful not to touch your eyes. Or wash your hands thoroughly afterwards.

Serves 3–4
Preparation and cooking time: 15 minutes

Stir-Fry Sauce: In a small bowl or cup combine 3 tbsp lime juice, 2 tbsp fish sauce and 1½ tbsp grated palm or soft brown sugar. Stir until the sugar dissolves and set aside.

4 tbsp oil
1 tbsp finely chopped garlic
4 hot red chillies, finely sliced
12 medium fresh prawns, shelled and deveined
½ tsp palm or soft brown sugar
4 cups steamed jasmine rice
3 tbsp fish sauce
2 tbsp lime juice
1 cup holy basil leaves
Extra sliced chilli to garnish (optional)

- Heat the oil in a wok or large pan over medium heat and fry the garlic and chillies for a few seconds until fragrant.

- Add the prawns and stir-fry until the prawns are cooked, about 3 minutes.

- Stir through the sugar, rice, fish sauce, lime juice and basil leaves. Stir-fry for a few minutes until hot.

- Serve garnished with extra chilli if using.

STIR-FRIED RICE WITH PINEAPPLE

The sweetness of the pineapple and the freshness of the cherry tomatoes in this recipe make for a lovely combination of textures and flavours. If they are in season, buy fresh pineapples and serve the rice in the pineapple shells to really impress.

Note: Be careful when handling the chilli as it will irritate the skin and eyes. Wear thin rubber gloves and be careful not to touch your eyes. Or wash your hands thoroughly afterwards.

Serves 3–4
Preparation and cooking time: 25 minutes

1 tbsp butter
2 tbsp oil
1 small onion, finely sliced
8 large prawns, shelled and de-veined
1 cup pineapple pieces, fresh or canned
1 hot red chilli, finely sliced
2 tsp Thai curry powder (page 83)
4 cups steamed jasmine rice
1 tsp palm or soft brown sugar
2 tbsp fish sauce
10 ripe cherry tomatoes, halved
2 tbsp chopped coriander leaves

- Heat the butter and oil in a wok or large pan over medium heat and fry the onion for 2–3 minutes until soft.

- Add the prawns and stir-fry for 2 minutes. Add the pineapple and stir-fry for a further 2–3 minutes or until the prawns are cooked.

- Add the chilli and curry powder and stir-fry for a few seconds, then add the rice, sugar and fish sauce. Stir-fry for a few minutes until hot.

- Add the tomatoes and coriander and stir though. Serve.

VEGETABLE FRIED RICE

This easy and nutritious fried rice is great as a side dish to mop up the sauce in fish or meat curries. Use any vegetables that are fresh and in season and add some tofu for a complete vegetarian meal.

Serves 4
Preparation and cooking time: 25 minutes

Stir-Fry Sauce: In a small bowl or cup combine 2 tbsp soy sauce, 1 tbsp fish sauce and 1 tsp ground white pepper.

4 tbsp oil
2 eggs, lightly beaten
1 onion, finely sliced
2 cloves garlic, finely chopped
1 small red capsicum, diced
1 small courgette (zucchini), diced
½ cup frozen peas
½ cup frozen corn kernels
4 cups steamed brown rice
2 spring onions, sliced into 2.5 cm (1 inch) pieces

- Heat 1 tbsp of the oil in a wok or large pan over high heat and swirl it around to coat the surface.

- Add the beaten egg and swirl that around so that you have a thinnish layer of egg. Cook until set. Remove from the pan and slice into strips.

- Heat the remaining oil in the same pan over medium heat and fry the onion and garlic for a minute or two until fragrant.

- Add the capsicum and stir-fry for a minute. Add the courgette, peas and corn and stir-fry for a further 2–3 minutes until the vegetables are cooked but not mushy.

- Add the sauce, rice and spring onions and stir-fry until everything is well combined and hot. Serve.

NOODLE DISHES

Consumed all over Asia, noodles are available in an abundant array of shapes and sizes and are made from a variety of ingredients such as rice, wheat, beans (mung), potato, millet and others. Tasty, filling, relatively cheap and simple to cook, noodles make a regular appearance in Thai cuisine.

THAI HERB FLAVOURED NOODLES

This easy and fresh tasting dish is great for vegetarian Thai food lovers.
Stir through some prawns or cooked chicken for non-vegetarians.

Serves 3–4
Preparation and cooking time: 35 minutes

Stir-Fry Sauce: In a small bowl or cup combine ½ cup vegetable stock,
3 tbsp fish sauce, 2 tbsp soy sauce, 2 tbsp sweet chilli sauce and 3 tbsp
lime juice.

300 g (10 oz) dried egg noodles
4 tbsp oil
2 eggs, lightly beaten
2 tbsp red curry paste (page 44)
½ cup roasted peanuts, roughly chopped
6 spring onions, sliced
1 cup bean sprouts
1 cup basil leaves
1 cup coriander leaves
½ cup mint leaves

To serve: fish sauce, hot sauce, lime wedges

- Cook the noodles in lightly salted boiling water until just tender.
  Drain, rinse in cold water and drain again.

- Heat about 2 tsp oil in a wok or large pan and add the egg. Stir
  until cooked like well done scrambled eggs and remove from the
  pan. Set aside.

- Add the remaining oil to the wok/pan and stir-fry the curry paste
  for a minute until fragrant. Add the noodles, toss and stir-fry for 2
  minutes and stir through the prepared sauce and egg.

- Add the remaining ingredients, toss to combine, turn off the heat and
  do the taste test. Add fish sauce, lime juice or sweet chilli sauce as
  desired.

BANGKOK STREET STYLE NOODLES

This simple but tasty noodle dish is inspired by the street vendors of Bangkok. Chinese influences are evident in the choice of fresh wheat noodles but the delicious flavours and aromas are unmistakably Thai.

Note: Be careful when handling the chilli as it will irritate the skin and eyes. Wear thin rubber gloves and be careful not to touch your eyes. Or wash your hands thoroughly afterwards.

Serves 3–4
Preparation and cooking time: 25 minutes

Stir-Fry Sauce: In a small bowl or cup combine 2 tbsp fish sauce, 3 tbsp oyster sauce, 1 tbsp lime juice, 2 tsp grated palm or soft brown sugar and 2 tsp cornflour dissolved in ½ cup of water. Stir until the sugar dissolves and set aside.

2 chicken fillets, sliced into strips
2 tbsp soy sauce
3 tbsp oil
4 cloves garlic, finely chopped
2 tsp grated galangal or ginger
1 small red chilli, finely sliced
1 cup smallish broccoli florets
½ cup mushrooms, sliced
3 spring onions, sliced into 2.5 cm (1 inch) lengths
450 g (1 lb) fresh wheat noodles
2 cups bean sprouts
½ cup Thai basil leaves, roughly torn
½ cup coriander leaves (optional)

To serve: lime wedges, fish sauce, hot chilli sauce

- Combine the chicken and soy sauce in a medium bowl and set aside whilst preparing the other ingredients.

- Heat the oil in a wok or large pan over medium heat and fry the garlic and galangal (or ginger) for a minute until aromatic.

- Turn up the heat, add the chicken and chilli and stir-fry for about 3 minutes or until the chicken is almost cooked.

- Add the broccoli, mushrooms and spring onions with about 2 tbsp water and stir-fry for a further 2 minutes until the broccoli is a bright green. Add another splash of water if the wok/pan is drying out too much during this time.

- Turn the heat down to medium and add the prepared sauce and noodles. Gently toss the noodles using two wooden spoons until everything is well combined and the noodles are cooked, about 3 minutes.

- Stir through the bean sprouts and basil leaves. Turn off the heat and do the taste test. Add fish sauce, lime juice or chilli as desired. Serve sprinkled with the coriander if using.

GINGER AND HONEY CHICKEN
WITH RICE NOODLES

This is a delicious and warming combination of gingery and sweet flavours. I often use thin rice noodles (also called rice vermicelli) for this dish but you can use any kind of rice noodles you like.

Note: Be careful when handling the chilli (if using) as it will irritate the skin and eyes. Wear thin rubber gloves and be careful not to touch your eyes. Or wash your hands thoroughly afterwards.

Serves 3–4
Preparation and cooking time: 30 minutes

Stir-Fry Sauce: In a small bowl or cup combine ½ cup runny honey, 2 tbsp soy sauce, 3 tbsp fish sauce and 2 tbsp lime juice

250 g (9 oz) dried rice noodles of choice
3 tbsp oil
1 onion, sliced
3 cloves garlic, finely sliced
2 tbsp grated ginger
1 red capsicum, thinly sliced
1 red chilli, finely sliced (optional)
450 g (1 lb) chicken thigh fillets, trimmed and sliced
1 cup mushrooms, sliced
4 spring onions, sliced into 2.5 cm (1 inch) lengths

To serve: lime wedges, fish sauce, hot chilli sauce

- Soak the rice noodles according to the packet instructions, drain and set aside.

- Meanwhile, heat a wok or pan over medium heat, add the oil and swirl to coat. Add the onion, garlic, ginger and capsicum and stir-fry for a minute.

- Add the chilli (if using), chicken and mushrooms and stir-fry for 3–4 minutes or until the chicken is cooked through. Add a splash of water if the wok/pan is drying out too much during this time.

- Stir in the prepared sauce, spring onions and noodles and carefully toss and stir using two wooden spoons until all the ingredients are well combined and heated through.

- Turn off the heat and do the taste test. Add fish sauce or lime juice as desired.

RICE NOODLES WITH PORK AND SWEET SOY SAUCE

This tasty and substantial noodle dish is a traditional Thai recipe usually made with fresh rice noodles. Dried noodles are a good alternative if you can't find fresh.

Note: Be careful when handling the chilli (if using) as it will irritate the skin and eyes. Wear thin rubber gloves and be careful not to touch your eyes. Or wash your hands thoroughly afterwards.

Serves 3–4
Preparation and cooking time: 32 minutes

Stir-Fry Sauce: In a small bowl or cup combine 2 tbsp oyster sauce, 2 tsp sweet soy sauce, 2 tbsp fish sauce, ½ tsp ground black pepper, 2 tsp grated palm or soft brown sugar. Stir until the sugar dissolves and set aside.

250 g (9 oz) dried flat rice noodles
3 tbsp cooking oil
4 cloves garlic, finely chopped
250 g (9 oz) pork fillet, thinly sliced
2 cups smallish broccoli florets (or vegetables of choice)
2 eggs, beaten
1 large red chilli, sliced (optional)

To serve: lime wedges, fish sauce, hot chilli sauce

- Soak the noodles in warm water for 20 minutes or according to the packet instructions, then drain.

- Meanwhile, heat a wok or large pan over medium heat and add about 2 tbsp of the oil. Swirl to coat and add the garlic and pork. Stir-fry for 2 minutes.

- Add the broccoli and a splash of water and stir-fry for a further 2 minutes.

- Stir in the noodles and toss and stir with two wooden spoons for 3–4 minutes or until the noodles are soft.

- Move the mixture to one side of the wok/pan and add the remaining oil. When hot, stir in the beaten egg and stir it for about 30 seconds until set.

- Bring all the ingredients together and stir-fry for a minute longer.

- Turn off the heat and do the taste test. Add more fish sauce or soy sauce as desired.

- Serve sprinkled with the chilli if using.

BROWN RICE NOODLES WITH PRAWN AND MUSHROOM

This recipe is healthy, tasty, quick and easy to prepare. Try it with a range of mushrooms and add some greens on the side for a complete meal.

Note: Be careful when handling the chilli as it will irritate the skin and eyes. Wear thin rubber gloves and be careful not to touch your eyes. Or wash your hands thoroughly afterwards.

Serves 3–4
Preparation and cooking time: 30 minutes

Stir-Fry Sauce: In a small bowl or cup combine 3 tbsp fish sauce, 2 tbsp oyster sauce, 1 tbsp sweet chilli sauce and 2 tbsp lime juice.

300 g (10 oz) thin brown rice noodles
3 tbsp oil
4 cloves garlic, finely sliced
12 king prawns, shelled with tails intact
½ cup straw mushrooms, sliced
½ cup oyster mushrooms, sliced
½ cup coriander leaves
1 long red chilli, sliced

To serve: lime wedges, fish sauce, hot chilli sauce

- Soak the noodles in warm water for 10 minutes or according to the packet instructions. Drain and plunge into cold water for a few seconds. Drain again and combine with 1 tbsp of the oil to prevent them sticking.

- Meanwhile, heat the remaining oil in a wok or large pan over medium heat and stir-fry the garlic for about 30 seconds.

- Add the prawns and mushrooms and stir-fry for 3–4 minutes or until the prawns are cooked.

- Add the hot noodles, pour over the prepared sauce and toss and stir with two wooden spoons until everything is well combined.

- Stir though the coriander, turn off the heat and do the taste test. Add fish sauce, sweet chilli sauce or lime juice as desired.

- Serve garnished with the chilli.

FRIED EGG NOODLES WITH BEEF AND WATER CHESTNUTS

The mint in this recipe gives the robust flavours a tasty lift. It is a satisfying dish for healthy appetites.

Note: Be careful when handling the chilli as it will irritate the skin and eyes. Wear thin rubber gloves and be careful not to touch your eyes. Or wash your hands thoroughly afterwards.

Serves 3–4
Preparation and cooking time: 35 minutes

Stir-Fry Sauce: In a small bowl or cup combine ½ cup beef stock, 2 tbsp fish sauce, 1 tbsp soy sauce, 1 tbsp oyster sauce, 1 tbsp lime juice or vinegar and 1 tbsp grated palm or soft brown sugar. Stir until the sugar is dissolved and set aside.

230 g (8 oz) lean beef, sliced into thin strips
1 tbsp soy sauce
1 tsp cornflour
4 cloves garlic, finely sliced
300 g (10 oz) flat egg noodles
3 tbsp oil
½ cup straw mushrooms, thinly sliced
6 Shiitake mushrooms, soaked and sliced
1 cup water chestnuts, sliced
2 tsp roast chilli paste (page 52)
½ cup mint leaves
1 large red chilli, sliced

To serve: fish sauce, lime wedges and hot chilli sauce

- Combine together the beef, soy sauce, cornflour and garlic and set aside whilst preparing the rest of the ingredients.

- Cook the noodles in lightly salted boiling water for about 10 minutes or until tender. Drain and mix with a little of the oil to stop them from sticking together.

- Heat a wok or large pan over high heat, add the oil and swirl to coat. Add the beef and marinade and stir-fry for a minute or two until the meat is sealed.

- Turn down the heat a little and add the mushrooms. Stir-fry for 2 minutes.

- Stir in the water chestnuts, chilli paste, noodles and prepared sauce. Toss and stir using two wooden spoons until well combined and heated through.

- Stir through the mint leaves, turn off the heat and do the taste test. Add fish sauce, sugar or chilli as desired.

- Serve, garnished with the sliced chilli.

SPICY SALADS

A Thai salad is a delicious and refreshing combination of flavours and textures. A typical Thai meal generally includes a spicy salad served with several other dishes. Traditionally these salads are very hot and sour, but the recipes in this book tone down these flavours a little to suit western tastebuds.

SPICY PORK AND LEMONGRASS SALAD

A very hot and sour salad that is bursting with lip smacking flavours. Fresh lemongrass and hot chillies are integral to this dish and are used in generous quantities. You might need to reduce the quantities of each if you don't like very hot food. Chicken breast can be used instead of pork if you wish.

Serves 2–3
Preparation and cooking time: 25 minutes

450 g (1 lb) pork fillet, trimmed and thinly sliced
8 tbsp finely sliced lemongrass, fresh or frozen, white part only
200 ml (6 fl oz) lime juice
1 tsp salt
6 hot chillies, finely sliced (see page 136)
4 tbsp fish sauce
2 tsp grated palm or soft brown sugar
8 kaffir lime leaves, shredded (or 2 tsp grated lime zest)
½ cup lemon basil leaves

To serve: steamed jasmine rice, fish sauce, hot sauce,
    lime wedges, white sugar

- Combine the pork with half the lemongrass, half the lime juice, and all the salt. Set aside for 10–15 minutes.

- Combine all the remaining ingredients except the basil leaves in a cup or small bowl and stir to dissolve the sugar.

- Do the taste test and add more fish sauce, lime juice or sugar as needed. The flavours should be strong as they will be diluted a little when added to the pork.

- Heat a dry wok over medium heat and add the pork. Stir-fry for 2–3 minutes until just cooked.

- Arrange the pork on a serving plate, spoon over the dressing, sprinkle with basil leaves and serve.

THAI CHICKEN SALAD

This delicious, intensely flavoured salad (laab), which can be made with pork or beef as well as chicken, is a favourite with Thais and westerners alike. It is usually served at room temperature although I have eaten it warm in Thai restaurants. Try it both ways to see which you like best.

The toasted ground rice really helps bring it together and gives it its unique flavour and texture, so do try and use it if you can.

Note: Be careful when handling chillies as they will irritate the skin and eyes. Wear thin rubber gloves and be careful not to touch your eyes. Or wash your hands thoroughly afterwards.

Serves 2–3
Preparation and cooking time: 20 minutes

1 tbsp oil
450 g (1 lb) minced chicken
4 large cloves garlic, very finely sliced
1 stick celery, sliced
2–3 hot red chillies, finely sliced
1 tbsp grated galangal or ginger
3 tbsp fish sauce
2 tsp grated palm or soft brown sugar
½ cup lime juice
1 cup bean sprouts
2 spring onions, sliced
2 tbsp toasted ground rice (Khao Kua Pon)
½ cup mint leaves
½ cup coriander leaves
½ an iceberg lettuce, torn into bite sized pieces

To serve: steamed jasmine rice, hot chilli sauce, fish sauce,
    lime wedges

- Heat the oil in a wok or large pan over medium heat and stir-fry the chicken for about a minute until opaque.

- Add half the garlic and stir-fry for a minute. Add the celery and stir-fry for a further minute. The celery should still be crisp. Cool slightly.

- In a medium bowl, combine the remaining garlic, chillies, galangal (or ginger), fish sauce, sugar and about three-quarters of the lime juice. Stir until the sugar dissolves and mix through the bean sprouts and spring onion.

- Add the warm chicken mixture and mix well. Set aside for a few minutes to cool and absorb the flavours.

- Do the taste test and add more chilli, fish sauce, lime juice or sugar as required to get a nice balance of flavours.

- Stir through the ground rice, mint and coriander leaves. Serve piled onto a bed of iceberg lettuce and serve.

Tip: *If you can't find toasted rice powder at your Asian shop or supermarket it is easy to make at home. Heat a heavy based frying pan and toss in ½ cup or so of jasmine or sticky rice. Keep the rice moving around until it is nicely browned. Cool and grind to a powder using a spice or coffee grinder. Store what you don't use in a dry airtight container.*

THAI BEEF SALAD

Delicious as part of a banquet or on its own as a light meal on a warm summer evening, this hot and spicy salad is really quick and easy. Use more or less chilli according to taste.

Note: Be careful when handling chillies as they will irritate the skin and eyes. Wear thin rubber gloves and be careful not to touch your eyes. Or wash your hands thoroughly afterwards.

Serves 2–3
Preparation and cooking time: 20 minutes

450 g (1 lb) steak, rump or sirloin
3 large cloves garlic, pounded to a paste
4–8 hot red chillies, de-seeded and finely sliced
2 tsp grated palm or soft brown sugar
4 tbsp fish sauce
2 limes juiced
½ red onion, sliced
½ cup mint leaves
½ red capsicum, thinly sliced
½ iceberg or cos lettuce, torn into bite sized pieces
½ cup coriander leaves
1 tbsp chopped roasted peanuts (optional)

To serve: steamed jasmine rice, hot sauce, fish sauce,
    lime wedges

- Grill or barbecue the steak until medium rare or cooked to your liking. Set aside to rest for a few minutes.

- Meanwhile, combine the garlic, chillies, sugar, fish sauce and about three-quarters of the lime juice in a medium bowl. Stir until the sugar is dissolved.

- Trim the steak while still warm, slice thinly and add to the bowl with the onion, mint and capsicum. Toss to combine and set aside to absorb the flavours.

- Do the taste test and add more chilli, lime juice, fish sauce or sugar as required until you have the right balance of flavours.

- Serve the beef arranged on a bed of lettuce, garnished with coriander leaves and peanuts if using, and accompanied by steamed jasmine rice.

WARM PRAWN SALAD

This is a fabulous dish that can be made with lobster, crab, scallops or any firm fish of your choice. Or try a combination of seafood for a real treat.

Note: Be careful when handling chillies as they will irritate the skin and eyes. Wear thin rubber gloves and be careful not to touch your eyes. Or wash your hands thoroughly afterwards.

Serves 4
Preparation and cooking time: 30 minutes

1 stalk lemongrass, pale part only, finely sliced
  (or equivalent of frozen)
3–4 hot red chillies, de-seeded and finely sliced
2 limes, juiced
1 tsp finely grated lime zest
3 tbsp fish sauce
2 tsp grated palm or soft brown sugar
1 kg (2.2 lb) king prawns, shelled with tails left intact
½ cup mint leaves
½ cup coriander leaves
2 spring onions, sliced on the diagonal
10 cm (4 inch) piece cucumber, peeled and thinly sliced
2 cups baby spinach leaves
1 tbsp oil

To serve: steamed jasmine rice, fish sauce, hot sauce,
  lime wedges

- In a small bowl or cup combine the lemongrass, chillies, lime juice and zest, fish sauce and sugar. Stir until the sugar dissolves.

- Do the taste test and add more chilli, lime juice, fish sauce or sugar until you have the right balance of flavours.

- Place the prawns in a ceramic bowl and pour over half of the dressing. Stir well, cover and set aside for 10–15 minutes.

- Meanwhile, combine the remaining dressing with the mint leaves, coriander, spring onion and cucumber.

- Place the spinach leaves on a serving plate and top with the herb and cucumber mixture.

- Heat the oil in a wok or pan and stir-fry the prawns for 3–4 minutes until just cooked.

- Arrange the prawns on top of the herb and cucumber mixture and serve immediately.

THAI GREEN MANGO SALAD

The delicious flavours and textures of this wonderfully healthy salad are nothing short of amazing. Sometimes made with green papaya and served heaped over barbecued chicken or crispy fried fish, it is commonplace in Thailand's food markets and good Thai restaurants.

Serves 4 as a side dish
Preparation time: 20 minutes

Spicy Dressing: In a small bowl or cup combine 4 tbsp fish sauce, 4 tbsp lime juice, 2 tsp tamarind paste, 1 finely sliced hot red chilli and 2 tsp grated palm or soft brown sugar. Stir until the tamarind and sugar dissolve and set aside.

3 cups peeled and grated green mango
1 cup bean sprouts
1 red onion, sliced
1 cup mint leaves
½ cup coriander leaves
1 tbsp crispy fried onion (optional)

To serve: grilled chicken or crispy fried fish, steamed rice

- Place all the ingredients except for the crispy fried onion in a medium bowl, add the dressing and toss to combine.

- Do the taste test and add chilli, fish sauce, lime juice or sugar as needed to get the right intensity and balance of flavours.

- Transfer to a serving plate and sprinkle over the crispy fried onion just before serving

THAI CUCUMBER SALAD

It is a common and welcoming practice in Thailand to serve cooling and refreshing accompaniments such as this lovely sweet and sour cucumber salad with hot curries and satays. It's really easy to make and very versatile.

Note: Be careful when handling the chilli (if used) as it will irritate the skin and eyes. Wear thin rubber gloves and be careful not to touch your eyes. Or wash your hands thoroughly afterwards.

Serves 4–6 as an accompaniment
Preparation and cooking time: 20 minutes

1½ cups white vinegar
1 tsp salt
3 tbsp white sugar
2 cups thinly sliced cucumber (peeled if desired)
1 tbsp chopped coriander leaves
1 tbsp diced red capsicum
1 spring onion, finely sliced
1 red chilli, de-seeded and sliced (optional)

- Combine the vinegar, salt and sugar in a small saucepan and bring to the boil, stirring, until the sugar dissolves. Cool.

- Place all the remaining ingredients in a bowl and pour over the cooled vinegar and sugar mixture. Serve immediately to enjoy the crisp freshness of the salad ingredients.

THAI DESSERTS

A great Thai meal is not complete without a sweet and scrumptious dessert. Whether it's a fragrant fruit salad in a sweetly spiced sugar syrup, a delectable and cooling ice-cream or a luscious creamy custard, a Thai dessert is a welcome conclusion to a fiery meal.

Thai desserts are generally low in fat and high in nutrition and flavour so everyone can enjoy a sweet ending to their meal.

EXOTIC FRUIT SALAD

A light, colourful and refreshing dessert of lovely summer fruit, this will cool you down and provide the perfect ending to your meal. Use the freshest, sweetest fruit you can find for optimum results and, if you really want to make an impression, serve the salad in hollowed out pineapple or melon shells.

Serves 4–6
Preparation and cooking time: 20 minutes
(plus cooling time)

1½ cups white sugar
1½ cups water
1 tbsp lime juice
1 strip lime rind
1 star anise (optional)
1 cup pawpaw chunks
1 cup lychees, peeled and seeded
1 cup pineapple chunks
1 cup melon chunks
1 cup watermelon chunks
1 star fruit, sliced
Sprigs of mint to garnish

- Place the sugar and water in a small pan and stir over medium heat without boiling until the sugar has completely dissolved.

- Add the lime juice and rind and bring to the boil. Simmer for 10 minutes. Turn off the heat and add the star anise if using. Cool.

- Once cooled strain the syrup into a suitable container and refrigerate until required.

- Meanwhile, place the fruit in a bowl and chill for about 30 minutes.

- When ready to serve, pour the syrup over the fruit, toss gently to combine and serve garnished with a sprig of mint.

COCONUT CUSTARD WITH SPICED CARAMEL SAUCE

An elegant, delicious and healthy Thai version of crème caramel, this lovely dessert is incredibly easy to make. It is scrumptious on its own or with fresh tropical fruit.

Serves 4
Preparation and cooking time: 45 minutes

1 cinnamon stick
2 cloves
¼ tsp ground nutmeg
2 tbsp soft brown sugar
150 ml (5 fl oz) water
150 ml (7 fl oz) coconut milk
100 ml coconut cream
1 tbsp caster sugar
Pinch of salt
2 eggs

- Pre-heat the oven to 160°C/140°C fan/325°F/gas mark 3. Lightly grease 4 x ½ cup ramekins or cups.

- Place the cinnamon stick, cloves, nutmeg, sugar and water in a small pan and stir over low heat until the sugar dissolves.

- Bring to the boil and boil for about a minute until slightly reduced and syrupy. Cool and strain the syrup into a small jug. Set aside.

- Meanwhile, warm the coconut milk, coconut cream and caster sugar and pinch of salt, stirring until the sugar has dissolved.

- Break the eggs into a medium bowl and beat until frothy. Pour in the warm milk and cream mixture and mix well.

- Pour 1 tablespoon of syrup into each ramekin – there should be enough to coat the bottom completely.

- Pour the egg and coconut mixture into each ramekin until about three-quarters full. Place the ramekins in a deep baking dish.

- Pour enough hot water into the baking dish to reach half way up the ramekins and bake in the oven for about 35 minutes or until a knife inserted into the custard comes out clean.

- Allow to cool and refrigerate until required. To serve invert each custard onto a serving plate.

STICKY RICE WITH MANGO

This classic Thai dessert of sweet rice in creamy coconut milk, topped with fresh, sweet fragrant mangoes, is a must for mango lovers. And it is also easy to prepare.

Serves 3–4
Preparation and cooking time: 35 minutes
(plus soaking time)

1 cup Thai sweet rice (also called glutinous or sticky rice)
1¾ cups water
100 ml (5 fl oz) coconut milk
¼ tsp salt
100 ml coconut cream
¼ cup grated palm or brown sugar
1 or 2 ripe mangoes, sliced
Fresh mint sprigs, to garnish

- Wash the rice in several changes of water and drain. Add the water to the rice and allow it to soak for at least 20 minutes, or overnight.

- Transfer the rice and water to a medium saucepan, add about a quarter of the coconut milk, a pinch of salt and slowly bring to a simmer stirring frequently.

- Simmer over low heat, covered, for about 20 minutes until all the liquid is absorbed. Turn off the heat and let the rice steam for 10 minutes. Transfer to a large bowl and gently fluff the rice up with a fork.

- Meanwhile, place the remaining coconut milk, half the coconut cream, another pinch of salt and the sugar in a small saucepan and heat, stirring, over low-medium heat for about 5 minutes, until the sugar is dissolved and the milk is very hot. Do not boil.

- Slowly pour the heated coconut milk over the rice and, using a fork, gently break the rice up into small lumps. Do not stir it as it will become soggy. Allow the mixture to rest for a few minutes.

- To serve, place mounds of the rice into the centre of serving bowls, arrange the mango slices around the mounds and drizzle over a little coconut cream. Garnish with some mint sprigs.

ORANGES IN ROSE-SCENTED SYRUP

This sweet, fragrant dessert of fresh, juicy orange segments couldn't be easier to make and is ideal to put out the fire on your tastebuds after a tantalizingly hot meal.

It's easy to segment the oranges: using a small sharp paring knife simply peel whole oranges removing all skin and pith. Then taking an orange in the palm of your hand and holding it over a bowl, slide the knife between the flesh and membrane on each side of each segment until the segment falls away. Repeat until all the segments have been removed and squeeze out any remaining juice left in the membrane over the orange segments.

Serves 4–6
Preparation and cooking time: 20 minutes
(plus cooling time)

1 cup white sugar
1½ cups water
1 tsp rosewater
6 oranges, segmented
Sprigs of mint to garnish

- Place the sugar and water in a small saucepan and stir over medium heat without boiling until the sugar is completely dissolved.

- Bring the syrup to the boil and boil for about 5 minutes until thickened slightly. Cool.

- Stir the rosewater into the syrup and combine with the orange segments. Chill for at least 30 minutes before serving, garnished with sprigs of fresh mint.

CREAMY COCONUT ICE-CREAM

Ice-cream is a popular, readily available snack and dessert throughout Thailand. Often served by bicycle and motorized cart vendors, it is made with coconut milk and does not generally contain any dairy cream at all. Nevertheless it is creamy, delicious and a cool ending to a spicy meal.

This recipe combines coconut and dairy milk and is really easy, particularly if you have an ice-cream maker.

Serves 8–10
Preparation and freezing time: About 30 minutes
with an ice-cream maker

225 ml (8 fl oz) sweetened condensed milk
800 ml (14 fl oz) coconut milk
1 tbsp fresh grated or desiccated coconut (optional)
Sprigs of mint to garnish

- Whisk all the ingredients except the desiccated coconut in a bowl until well combined and frothy.

- Place in the bowl of your ice-cream maker and prepare the ice-cream according to the manufacturer's instructions.

- If using desiccated coconut, sprinkle in during the last five minutes.

- Serve 2 to 3 scoops per person, decorated with a sprig of mint.

Tip: *If you don't have an ice-cream maker, add the desiccated coconut to the whisked mixture, stir well and transfer to a loaf tin or similar and place the mixture in the freezer. Remove from the freezer after 30 minutes and beat with a whisk or a fork until smooth. Repeat twice more and freeze until hard.*

CARAMELIZED BANANAS WITH ORANGE LIQUEUR

A remarkably easy and absolutely delicious sweet of ripe bananas smothered in sticky caramel sauce flavoured with orange liqueur.

Serves 4
Preparation and cooking time: 20 minutes

2 tbsp desiccated coconut
60 g (2 oz) butter
1½ tbsp soft brown sugar
½ tsp dried ginger
Grated zest of 1 orange (unwaxed)
Juice of ½ orange
4 tbsp orange liqueur
4 bananas, peeled and sliced lengthways
Slices of orange to garnish

To serve: cream or ice-cream

- Heat a small frying pan over medium heat and add the coconut. Cook, stirring, for about a minute until the coconut becomes lightly browned. Remove from the pan immediately and allow to cool.

- Melt the butter in a large non-stick frying pan and add the sugar, ginger, orange zest and juice. Stir over low heat until the sugar dissolves and the mixture starts to bubble.

- Add the orange liqueur and heat for a few seconds until bubbling again.

- Add the bananas, cut side down, and cook for a minute or so over medium heat. Turn to coat in the sauce and cook for a further minute.

- Serve the bananas on warmed serving plates, sprinkled with toasted coconut and garnished with the orange slices. Serve with cream or ice-cream.

INDEX